To Don and 'Rose[?]
may the happiness fairy
Bless you as she did Bless Us

Hoyt
Oct. 2005

# Rising Up
# Again and Again

## How Life Can Be Fun
## If You Want It To Be

## Horst Schneider

Wingspan Press

Printed in the United States of America.

Published by
WingSpan Press
Livermore, CA
www.wingspanpress.com

The WingSpan® name, logo and colophon are
the trademarks of WingSpan Publishing.

ISBN 1-59594-023-5
EAN 978-1-59594-023-0
First Edition 2005

Library of Congress Control Number: 2005930649

# ACKNOWLEDGEMENT

I wish to give special thanks to
**Andress**, who unmercifully pestered, cajoled, and inveigled me to have this book published.
**Doug**, who twisted many arms to presell a bunch of copies.
**Stephen**, who proofread the manuscript and made many good suggestions, which found their way into this book.
**Fina**, who helped in many ways, and even donated a ream of paper towards typing the manuscript.
My **Wife**, Lover, and Teammate, who patiently checked facts, places, and dates, losing ten pounds in the process.
My **Parents**, since they made it possible for this book to have an author.

✳ ✳ ✳

The Romans had a saying, that to be a man one had to have fathered a son, built a home, and written a book. I am happy to report that I am now a man.

# 1

# THE EARLY YEARS

We had just cleared the breakfast table when the phone rang. It was our longtime friend Bill. We chatted for a bit before he announced his real reason for the call.

"Horst," he said, "I know I have mentioned my son-in-law, Eddy, my daughter's husband, a few times to you. My daughter Helen and he just blew into town unannounced and they can stay just for this weekend. So I would very much like for you two to meet them, and vice versa. I had told them a bit about you two when Sally and I visited them in spring and they are chafing at the bit to meet you in person. When could we bring them over to meet you?"

"Bill," I answered, "you know that you are welcome any time. When would you like to come over?"

Horst Schneider

"How about right after dinner if it's OK with you. We both eat fairly early now that we are retired. Naturally, I hope you can tell them some of the stories of your life. They have absolutely no idea how different the times were when you grew up in Europe. And I know they want to hear how you managed to get started here with three kids and a wife, - and only 17 cents to your name.

I know they would love to hear your stories from you directly. I have sort of whetted their appetite with a few bits, but you are so much better at telling your stories, especially the many funny ones."

# 2

And that was why Bill and Sally, Eddy and Helen, and Margo and I, were the following day sitting in our living room after dinner with a glass of wine in our hands.

As to the wine, I had to admit that whoever had bought that bottle, had good taste in wine. Shouldn't have been a surprise, I had taught Bill a lot about wines during the last year. In fact, he told me several times that he was lucky to have met me. After all, how many people here in our small city have a friend who grew up in Germany's wine area. One who also loves to share his knowledge of wines. Especially if that's done by the 'hands-on' method!

Bill's son and daughter-in-law were indeed a charming couple. After the usual preliminaries Bill turned to Eddy and his daughter to tell them that Margo and I had worked as volunteers at Mesa Verde Natl. Park in Colorado, which Eddy and Helen had visited a year before.

He turned to me and said, "You tell him about your friend Begay, the one with the walking staff."

"You see," I began, turning to the young couple, "Begay was a full blooded Navajo. He worked at the

Mesa Verde Natl. Park also, and would drop in at our Ranger Station almost every day, just to 'chew the fat', he said. But I found out soon enough that he also had another reason. He would invariably beg me to tell him another story of our life. At any rate, we became good friends. I told my stories and he told me a bit about himself and his life on the reservation."

Bill faced his daughter and son-in-law and explained, "Begay had a very special expression, I think it was something like this: 'That Horst, he talk good story.' Wasn't that the way he phrased it, Horst?" he asked, turning back to me.

Yes, that was the exact phrase Begay used when he talked to the rangers or his friends at work. I always wondered how many of my stories Begay repeated to his friends, and how those stories changed when he told them.

"Bill, my friend, your memory is excellent as to how Begay expressed himself," I answered him. "But he was not the one with the walking staff. That was Clyde, another friend of mine.

Well, Begay was a very soft-spoken man, and at first I wondered if he was a shaman. This he denied, but he did hint that he helped many people who sought him out. So I still don't know what his standing was among his people. All I can say is that I sometimes felt as if he was right inside my thoughts. Not intrusively, you know, but soothingly, approvingly, making me glad to just sit near him. He also taught me a few phrases of Navajo. So now I can at least greet a Navajo in his own tongue, as well as say good-bye to him.

Now to Clyde, who also was a Navajo, a very smart

man with a College degree, however, he preferred to live on the reservation with his family. He was both a very modern man and at the same time a fairly traditional Navajo, holding on to the old values. I very much admired the man.

We worked at the Park for a number of years, together with another couple with whom we shared duties and happy moments. One of our duties was to prepare the amphitheater in the evening for the nightly ranger talk. There we were given the first fifteen minutes to talk about safety and other Park concerns. When Margo and I hung up our hats, so to speak, we had quite a surprise on the last day of our duty.

After my little speech I was told to stay on the stage for a few more moments so Clyde could present me with a big walking staff. It turned out to be a very special gift.

This staff had been to all the ruins Clyde had gone to, and in each ruin he had whittled away some of the wood, leaving the shavings there. I guess I now carry with me not just wonderful memories of the Mesa Verde National Park, but also a small piece of the soul of some of the old, abandoned ruins."

Bill interrupted me, pointing a finger at my chest for emphasis. "You should really write this all down. After all, you are the first generation of your clan. You two came to America to start a new life for yourself and your children. Don't you think that your grandchildren, and the generations after them, would be very grateful later on if you did this? I am sure they would love to know where they came from, what life was like at that time, and in general who their forefathers were."

He was right. I had often wondered what kind of stories my grandfathers could have told. But they didn't have a word processor and so I will never know.

I agreed with him, "maybe I should do that some day. After all, that's what I have my word processor for. But let me ask you, which of our stories do you want me to tell?"

Bill chuckled as if I had made a good joke. "Now let's see," he said. "I am sure I have not heard all of them. So, you might as well just rattle along till you run out of steam or we have to leave. And if I have a choice, I would love for you to start by telling us about your youth, and what life was like then. That OK with you?"

I had had an idea that he was going to ask me to do that. So I just turned to the young couple. "Let me explain something you should know," I started. "To us it feels as if we had lived three lives. Going from one life to another is like stepping through a fog curtain. We know there is something behind the curtain, and we know also that it is very different.

First there was the pre-Hitler time, which was followed by Hitler's Germany, both before and during the war. After that came the postwar period, a miserable time. And finally there was our new life here in America.

Each life had different values and ideas and traditions. This was often confusing, and sometimes could lead to some embarrassment, and sometimes to hilarious misunderstandings, especially after we came to America.

Here in America we found new customs, many so different from the Old World. In fact, we had to change our way of thinking and how to look at the world. We had to change the way we interacted with people, the way we behaved in public.

Maybe an example or two might help. Let's say, Helen, you are being complimented about your dress. As a German you would not have said, 'Thank you', you would have belittled it with something like, 'Oh it is so old I am about to discard it.'

Here is another good one. In 1969 we visited Margo's brother in Germany. I went to pick up my rental car and quietly lined up behind the lone customer at the desk. Several Germans arrived shortly on my right and my left, calling the clerks, 'Hallo, Fräulein.' Whoa, I had forgotten, we don't stand in line. But it gets better.

The following Sunday morning Margo, her brother, and I went to a bakery. When we came to an intersection Margo and I stepped off the curb since there was no traffic for a mile in either direction. Her brother held us back and said, 'you can't walk now, the light is red.' At that moment it dawned on me. We Germans had been taught strict obedience, but not discipline. Here in the States, we generally exercise discipline, but not too much obedience.

Now let me show you what life was like in the Old Country for us when we grew up in the twenties and thirties. I'll start by giving you just a few tidbits of how different life was then, compared to today. The best way to do this, might be to tell you about our early life. Now, I do know that you are waiting for some of those funny stories, but be patient, I will get to them soon.

And since I can talk better with a full glass, let us attend to that first."

All of us, except Margo, poured some more of Bill's wine. And so fortified I continued.

# 3

"I myself had much freedom, but Margo had very little. For her there was not even outside play after school. She was not allowed to have friends visit her. Her life was strict and structured.

Let me tell you, Margo always has been a rebel, even at that young age. Instead of following in others' footsteps she thought for herself. And believe me, judging by the stories I heard from her, she did quite well in this respect. She was always headstrong with a mind of her own. In a way it was good training for later life. So she learned at an early age to cope with life's unpleasant problems.

Margo's youth and mine were maybe not the best, but somehow we survived. There is no question about it, life is a do-it-yourself job. And no one else can be held responsible for your happiness and fulfillment. You have to make that yourself.

Margo's mother died very young when Margo was just a baby. So Margo and her two brothers were farmed out to various relatives. Then, three years after her mother's death, her father married his housekeeper's sister. It was not a marriage of love but strictly convenience. He wanted to have his family together again and needed someone to bring up three kids.

The lady did the best she could. But she was a harsh and unfeeling woman who viewed life as a time of misery. She did not read, play, enjoy music, or engage in anything that even remotely reeked of fun. That in her eyes was a waste of time.

Her life was cooking, dusting, doing laundry, and waxing floors, on her hands and knees naturally. Just as potatoes had to be peeled standing up. This was dictated by tradition, which did not allow one to sit down when working in the kitchen. Margo being Margo, naturally did not go along with these stupid traditions. Therefore she was always chased out of the kitchen.

Margo had many problems with her stepmother. And I have no doubt that it worked both ways. One typical example were the darts. All the dresses, which her stepmother sewed for Margo, were naturally of the most plain variety.

So, when Margo was about thirteen or fourteen, she decided that as a girl she should show a bit of a figure. Soon her dresses sported little darts in the right spots. But after laundry day her stepmother would rip them out and Margo would sew them in again the next day.

Finally her stepmother told Margo, 'if you don't like what I make for you, you can sew your own.' But she didn't figure that Margo would do exactly that. Needless to say, from then on Margo made her own dresses.

As I said, she had a mind of her own and followed the path she perceived as the right one.

Her stepmother did not enjoy reading and could

not understand that Margo wanted to read. So Margo had to hide her books away in many odd places in the apartment where they could not be found easily. Whenever her stepmother caught Margo reading, Margo was reprimanded for wasting her time. But read she did, any time she had a free moment.

I might as well mention here also that Margo is dyslexic. This caused her much grief in school. Se was labeled as dumb since she often turned letters around when writing. Also, she did not read as fast as the other students. Dyslexia was not yet known at that time.

One more problem for her was the fact that she always was trying to use her left hand for writing and other activities. Many a ruler came down on her knuckles, while she was in school, to teach her the right way of doing things. It sure was a different time in history.

In Margo's house there were no loving hugs or kisses given out. Her father came from a medium well to do farmer's family in northern Germany, an area called Westphalia. The people from that region were well known to be frugal, industrious, and rather taciturn.

True, her father showed all those traits, but he could on occasion also be the center of the party. Especially, when he recited from memory one of the many funny, humorous poems he knew so well.

He was upright and honest, somewhat plodding at times, and strict in his old-fashioned dictatorial German way. But I will say this for him, he could also sometimes let a minor, or even not so minor, transgression slide past if he judged that he himself might have done the same.

You might think that Margo's parents were completely without feeling. That is not true, it was just another time in history. The values were different from today's. I am sure their views would have been much more tolerant had they lived at a different time. As it was, Margo's father just could not openly show his love for his daughter. This simply wasn't done where he came from.

Let me show you more of how different the times were. One day, when she was sixteen, Margo became violently ill on her way home. She stopped at a nearby doctor's office, and it turned out that she had advanced appendicitis. So she was immediately admitted to the hospital for an operation.

When her parents came the next day they let Margo know that she was not going to spoil their vacation plans. And with this they left, leaving Margo alone in the hospital and to fend for herself afterwards. It was a good thing that she had me by her side.

Even after she finished school and went to work at fourteen, she never saw her paycheck. Her paycheck was sent home to her parents. They then would dole out a few marks to Margo for streetcar fare etc. It was only after she turned twenty-one that she finally had access to her earnings. Until then her pocket money consisted of what she saved taking a one-hour walk from or to her job, instead of riding the streetcar.

It was no wonder then that she kept her private life to herself. She hardly ever confided in her parents about what happened in her life. Even after she had a very traumatic experience of gang rape at the age of twelve, she kept quiet. She knew what the answer would have been. In her mind she could hear her parents telling her that she should be ashamed, and that she probably had provoked the rape attack herself. At any rate, it was surely all her fault. As you can see, the values of that time were so different from today's. There just is no comparison.

The first one to hear her story was I after we had fallen in love. There was no way she told me right at the start that we could get serious. After all, a guy couldn't possibly get serious with a girl like her. It took some heavy talking on my part to have her discard the heavy baggage she had been carrying for the last four years.

When she told me about her traumatic experience it brought back some memories of my own. It had happened to me in a city south of Hamburg. I lived there in an orphanage for some time. You probably get the drift; I had had a similar encounter. There was a huge difference, though. The authorities told my mother about it, and as a result I was sent to live with some foster parents.

At any rate, these experiences did not traumatize our psyche, and maybe brought us even closer together, if that was possible. Boy, we really were in love, and we still are, and I don't know of anything that could change that.

Maybe I am talking too much about our youth, but how else can I tell you about the times they call the 'good old days'. So let me talk a bit about myself; and I'll try to make it less serious.

# 4

As a kid I lived in many places, first with my uncle, then in an orphanage, and after that with foster parents. For some time I even lived with Catholic monks in a monastery, but never with a father.

Now you may ask the question, how do we today feel about our youth. Did we have a good youth, or a bad one? Well, we do not feel that our youth was bad, it was just not what we would have wished for.

Are there any feelings of ill will towards our parents? Not at all. They acted out their life to the best of their ability, never to spite anyone. And they were convinced at the time that they had done their best. It was much later, in fact, shortly before they died that my mother, as well as Margo's stepmother, voiced some regrets.

I myself think I did have a very good youth, maybe not by your present standards. Hurdles and problems can either leave scars or can make you strong. As I said before, life is a do-it-yourself job.

My early memories are from the mid 1920s in Saarbrücken, a city in the West of Germany, just north of Alsace, France. My mother and father had divorced early on. So I lived with my mother, her brother, and my grandmother. They had a small four-room apartment on the third floor.

My mother's brother was an architect who had a multiplication machine, which always fascinated me tremendously. This fascinating machine could do numbers when you turned a crank. I remember watching my uncle using this contraption and finally I figured out how to use it. That's how I learned my numbers because he let me work with it when he was present."

"That's interesting," said Eddy, "that must have been sort of like a mechanical abacus. I never heard of that. And he let you play with it? That's amazing."

"Maybe you could describe it as a mechanized abacus. It had a lot of little gears that whirred around. And it also had some levers you had to set. At any rate it was a marvel as far as I was concerned.

But the most fascinating object was my uncle's huge encyclopedia. I spent many happy hours with those twenty-four volumes. Fact is, they helped me teach myself to read. Having to stay away from them was always the worst punishment my mother could dish out for any of my misdeeds.

But then came my first school year and it was absolute misery. There I was supposed to again learn to read and do numbers. But now I had to do that according to the strict and structured German school system of that time.

I loved my uncle dearly and did not realize that I had another uncle until a few years later, when my mother farmed me out to an orphanage. This was in 1929, in a city not too far south of Hamburg.

At that time my mother worked in Hamburg and she wanted me close, but maybe not too close. From time to time she would send me money to buy a train ticket to come to Hamburg and visit her.

Her brother Hugo also lived in Hamburg with his girlfriend. She was from Finland, a pretty and sweet person. I said my uncle lived in Hamburg. Actually, he was not home in Hamburg very often. He was a captain of a tramp steamer, traveling all over the world, from harbor to harbor. I remember him as a very imposing man who definitely commanded respect. I also remember him as an inveterate practical joker.

I very much admired his tea service, which he had brought with him from Japan. That tea set was absolutely beautiful. It was adorned with fanciful and colorful pictures, and dragons, and other imaginary beings, and it had a wide gold rim. The first time I was allowed to drink from this fine china, I almost choked. The gold rim was overlaid with hot Chinese mustard.It also did not take me long to learn that my uncle knew, which pralines were safe, and which were full of pepper or some other bothersome ingredient.

It was also not safe to use the toilet unless you first inspected the seat closely. Some people didn't, and as a result found themselves glued on to the seat.

But he had his redeeming traits also. Every time, after he had left for another trip, his girlfriend would run across treasures where there had not been any before. Maybe a pearl necklace in a cooking pot, maybe a hundred mark note at the bottom of the sugar bowl, another one tucked away in the dust cloth, and who knows where and what else.

Once my mother and I were invited to his ship. When we reached the water's edge in the harbor, he whistled sharply, and soon a small dinghy was on its way. As we were sculled to his ship we encountered annoying waves of tugboats and other craft. Our little boat rocked from side to side; it would dip one moment, and then rise the next. But my uncle stood unperturbed on one of the two wooden seats, a steady rock in a watery earthquake. My mother and I held on to him for dear life since we could not sit down. There were several inches of dirty water slopping around in the boat.

We finally made it. My uncle excused himself, telling us that he had some other business to attend to, and that we shouldn't have any difficulty finding our way. First we had to climb up the side of a barge, cross it, jump across to a second barge, and cross it. Once across we were tossed a rope ladder we had to climb up to the deck.

It was not easy, the rope ladder had nothing to hold the rope away from the side of the ship. My mother's knuckles, as well as mine, were raw by the time we reached the top. There we encountered one more obstacle, we had to climb over the railing. There was not one sailor anywhere in sight to help us.

My uncle, who had excused himself, suddenly appeared on the other side of the ship. Immediately several sailors materialized out of nowhere on that side. A rope ladder with nice wooden offsets was tossed down. And just before my uncle reached the deck a seaman jumped to the railing and swung open a gate in the railing. My uncle stepped on board to the shrill tone of a whistle. He looked quite unruffled.

Later he explained to my mother that it was customary that a ship's captain was piped on board. 'If you had just waited a bit when I told you that I had some other business to attend to,' he said with a most innocent face, 'you could have come up with me. It would have been much easier using my ladder than the old one on the other side. But you had to be hasty, it's your fault if you scraped your fingers.'

Sally couldn't hold back anymore. "Thanks, Horst, that was a new one. This one you have not told before. I hope you will tell us more of the funny ones, like the one with you and your mother in the streetcar."

"Don't worry," I assured her, "I will. You know I enjoy telling stories, and I like especially the funny ones.

But let's get back to when I was about five. After all, you wanted me to tell Helen and Eddie a bit about the 'good old times' that they luckily missed. Sure, I have wonderful memories, but I certainly would not like to live under those conditions again.

# 5

Unlike Margo, I had a lot of freedom to do and explore, it was almost as if I was treated like a semi-adult. I recall many happy hours on the Saar River with my uncle's two-seater foldboat, a kayak like boat. It was covered with real Rhino hide.

Some Sundays my uncle would phone the place where he kept the boat and ask the attendant to put it into the water for me. I would then take off for the French border. There I would eat my lunch, and then make the journey backwards. This was quite a journey for a five/six year old by himself in a two-seater kayak. And I loved it.

Another illustration of my freedom I vividly recall, happened in 1926, when my mother was transferred to work in Cologne. Once she was given a long weekend off, and called my uncle to have him send me to visit her. He gave me the fare amount plus a little change. And with that I went by streetcar to the train station where I bought my ticket, and then took the next train to Frankfurt. There I had to switch to the express to Cologne, where I arrived in the evening.

I had expected my mother to meet me at the train. When she was not there, I negotiated with a taxi driver to drive me to her address. I told him that he would be paid when we got there. My mother paid him, and nothing more was said about it.

And to this day I still do not know why she was not at the station. Looking back it seems to me that that was not an important issue for me or for her.

Needless to say, I made it back to Saarbrücken again by myself. And neither my uncle, nor my mother, nor I, thought it unusual for a six year old to buy his train tickets by himself. Then find his way through busy major train stations and locate the right train. It was a good thing I had taught myself to read.

My mother was a rather unusual person. It was no wonder that her marriage was a short-lived affair, she was much too strong willed, domineering, and capricious. She also could be extremely vindictive and spiteful at times. She once told me gleefully how she had opened the windows on a windy day, while my father was sorting his stamp collection, so his precious stamps could take flight down the street.

And from my uncle I heard the story of how my mother had one day cleared the furniture from the living room, took our hand wagon, and left for the nearby woods. There she collected fir branches, mosses, and leaf litter. When my father came home he walked into the woods instead of into his living room. The fir branches had been nailed to the walls and the leaf litter covered the floor.

She had even built a make believe campfire of logs in one corner of the room. It was complete with a light bulb behind some red crepe paper."

"That must have been quite a shock for your father," remarked Bill. He then turned to Sally and mockingly asked her: "What do you think I would have done in a situation like that." She just smiled and didn't answer. So I continued.

"You will have to admit that she was somewhat eccentric. In a way she was utterly unpredictable. But she was also a very strong and determined woman.

In 1925 she needed an income. But since she had not had a formal education, she did not find the kind of employment she wanted. So she decided to create her own job position. Now remember, this was the time when women as a rule could work only as nurses, as sales clerks, or as domestics.

First she bought a book on the then new subject of psychology and studied it. Next she went to the leading department store and told the manager that she should be hired to teach sales psychology to his sales staff. Naturally, she was turned down cold. But that manager was no match for my mother's determination and tenacity.

Her next step was to masquerade as a poor farmer's woman, complete with a wicker basket on her arm. At this time merchants did not display their wares openly as they do today, you had to ask for a shirt, let's say, and you were shown one shirt at a time. But still, my mother managed to steal so many items in one afternoon that her basket finally was full to the brim. With this evidence in hand she marched into the manager's office and now could convince him to hire her.

Those happenings should give you an idea how different the times were, when Margo and I were kids," I explained to Eddy and Helen. "Let me tell you a little more.

Up to the fall of 1935, the Saar Region was occupied by France. Our money was French, our Postal System was French, etc. The language naturally was German, although many people understood French also. It was a necessity.

This was a time when a man was not properly dressed unless he wore a hat on his head. But not so in the Saar Region. There, men went bareheaded for a simple reason. You see, when a German man encountered a French officer while walking along the street, he had to get off the sidewalk and doff his hat, showing respect. Rather than do that, the men went without hats and crossed the street or ducked into the nearest house entrance. The feeling between the Germans and the French was somewhat less than cordial.

# 6

My mother and I had our favorite spots to escape to on Sundays, such as the mountain right behind our apartment building, where I spent much time exploring. Other Sundays my mother and I would venture to the meadows up on top and collect salad greens the French call 'pis-en-lit' (pee in the bed), and we call dandelion. We often had dandelion salad with our evening meals.

Those meals were somewhat formal in my uncle's home, with sparkling wine glasses and linen napkins in silver napkin rings. My uncle or my mother would wind up the old Gramophone with the funnel shaped speaker, and we would listen to Caruso sing his arias. I wish I had this old Gramophone today.

Every afternoon a lady cook arrived to do some of the housework and cook the evening meal. She either must have been a very good cook, or a very cheap cook, because she stayed with us for many years.

I especially liked the way she prepared escargot, which she stuffed back into their shells, then topped them off with her special butter garlic and parsley sauce. Since there was no broiler, she used an old fry pan half filled with salt, to set the snail shells in and heat them. She then served them with a crisp salad and a French baguette. And to this day I still have my love for snails. They are still one of my favorite items on the menu.

But my most favorite Sunday spot was a large lake in the woods, at the end of the streetcar line. I was always eagerly looking forward to those Sunday trips. Not only because the area was beautiful, and the woods were cool and quiet, but also because of the entertainment later on the way home. And I cannot say which was the greater attraction to me.

Anyway, after making a trip around the lake, my mother and I would wander off the official path into the woods on a discovery trip. Everything had to be inspected, and some of the items had to be collected. For this my mother had thoughtfully emptied her big handbag before leaving home. By evening we usually had filled her bag with our treasures, and we would make our way back to the streetcar.

The streetcars of that period had two benches inside, one on either side of the coach, running the full length of the coach. This was also a time when chivalry was still practiced, males and kids would stand in the aisle, while the ladies occupied the benches. This was also a time when ladies wore long, full skirts, almost touching the ground.

Sunday evenings the streetcars were always packed to capacity. And a packed streetcar was what my mother needed for what she had in mind.

Once the packed streetcar was well on its way, my mother would surreptitiously open her handbag on the floor to let our motley collection escape. It was never very long before the first terrified shriek would hit us. And then pandemonium would break loose. Finally the streetcar would lurch to a halt. By this time all the women had frantically jumped up on the benches.

It usually took quite some time to collect all the confused little snakes, lizards, and frogs, and declare the premises safe again. There were also some accusing stares fired off in the direction of some of the boys present, but for once they were utterly innocent, or at least not completely guilty."

I turned to Sally. "I think that's the story you wanted to hear, right?"

"Horst," she sputtered, still laughing, "I have heard that story now twice before, but it makes me laugh every time again. You have so many funny ones, but this ranks right with the best. Makes me wonder now, which others you will tell us. I have a few suggestions, but I will keep my mouth shut."

"Thanks a bunch," I told her. "I will just have to surprise you.

But let's go on, I have sort of a travel plan in my head. That doesn't mean it's rigid. It's more like a very vague notion as to what I want to talk about to give you an idea of what the times were like and how Margo and I fitted in."

# 7

I have told you enough about my world, so now let's see how things looked in Margo's world.

The school year in Germany started right after Easter. So, when Margo was almost six years old, she was enrolled to start her first year of school in 1927. It lasted only a few days for her because she contracted Scarlet fever. That meant that she had to be quarantined at home.

There was an especially bad outbreak of Scarlet fever that year, a real epidemic that was sweeping the area. And when Margo finally returned to school after several weeks, only half of her classmates were still alive. You have to bear with me, because what follows leads up to the real story I want to tell you in a short while.

Being imprisoned in her room was not easy on a squirmy six-year-old girl. After all, even today our prisons use solitary confinement as penalty. Her father had to wear special clothes when entering her room, and he and the doctor were the only human visitors she had.

Fortunately for Margo, there were other visitors to keep her company and with whom she could play.

She fed them breadcrumbs, and eventually they became good buddies. Margo had always kept some marbles in her room, and these she would roll their way. They in turn would entertain Margo by playing with them.

As you can see, a bunch of mice were the only living companions she had for the several weeks that she was confined to her room. Margo called them her good friends. It's no wonder then that she thought that mice were cute and were great fun to watch. And as a result she never, even years later, had any fear of mice. On the contrary, she looked at mice as friends and playmates.

It was some time after the war that she told me this story. In fact, it must have been around 1946 or 1947, during a time when there was very little food in Germany. At this time we used to comb the nearby woods for mushrooms, berries, nuts, and wild vegetables.

One of the items we gathered were beechnuts. If you have never seen any, well, they are little bitsy things of which you need a hundred to make a small handful. It was slow work gathering them off the forest floor from among the fallen tree leaves.

But when she finally had enough to make it worth her while, she would take them to somebody in the village who had an oil press. After the nuts were pressed for oil, she was lucky if she maybe wound up with half a cupful of oil for many days of back stooping labor. A half cupful of oil at that time was a major, major treasure.

So, she always kept her precious beechnuts safely stashed away in an open square metal container in our room on the floor next to the door.

At this time we lived upstairs in a small room with just a straw bed for Margo and myself, and a small crib for our daughter Sigrid. There was also an old table and one rickety chair, and that was the extent of our furniture.

It must have been around midnight one night when I woke up. Bright moonlight was streaming through the open window and I could see Margo standing next to the door where she kept her metal canister with her precious beechnuts. When she noticed I was awake she turned to me and said accusingly, 'can you image the impertinence of this little rascal. There is a mouse in my beechnut canister!'

With that she quickly reached in, and then triumphantly held her hand out for me to see in the moonlight a little frightened, squeaking mouse. She went to the window and stood there for a moment, talking to her little friend.

'I am not going to kill you,' she told the mouse, 'but don't you dare ever come back'.

After she told the squeaking little critter never to come back, she tossed the little mouse out into the garden.

To me that was a perfect illustration of the old saying that bonds forged early in life are lasting bonds."

They all looked at Margo. And while the men laughed, Sally and Helen shook thcir heads. Sally muttered, "Margo, don't you dare ever to bring me one of your friends. It would be the last time you saw me." But we knew it was in jest.

It was time to explain. "You noticed that I made a time jump of about 20 years just now. Be prepared for more time jumps because I want to tell you my stories as they come to my mind, not in chronological order. But there will probably always be some connection."

# 8

I must have had a big grin on my face, when I turned to Eddy and Helen and asked, "would you like to hear how Margo and I met?" They both nodded and Helen even clapped her hands. Their answer was quick and short, "Oh, please do."

"Alright, I shall let you in on what is no secret," I laughed, "everyone else who knows us, seems to have heard it at one time or another. But first let's refill our glasses or would you rather have a cup of coffee?"

Everyone voted for coffee, so Margo jumped up and wheeled the little serving cart with the coffee, the cups, the sugar, and the cream into the middle of our circle. After a few sips of coffee I continued.

"Margo's father was a government employee with the Veterans Administration and in 1934 he was transferred to Berlin. While he went apartment hunting, he needed to stay somewhere, so when he heard that my mother had a room for rent in her apartment, he rented it for a few weeks.

Later, even after Margo's family had moved to Berlin into their new apartment, Margo's father still visited my mother from time to time. And that was how I met Margo. She was then about 14 and I saw her just once. I was absolutely not interested in that silly little girl at that time. And I certainly never dreamed of what would develop later.

About the time the family moved to Berlin, Margo left to work at a place, which in English can best be described as a Dude Ranch. I did not see that silly little girl again until two years later, when her brother Rudi decided to visit my mother. He took Margo along so she could meet my mother also. But as luck would have it, luck for us I mean, my mother was not home when he arrived with Margo in tow.

By this time my mother and I had moved into a smaller apartment, which was only two blocks walking distance from where Margo lived.

When Rudi rang the doorbell, I let them in and we sat down in the living room, Rudi to my left, and Margo facing me. Poor Rudi had to carry 100% of the conversation, because Margo and I just looked at each other. We were in love. And the rest is history. Come to think of it, this then actually would be love at second sight, wouldn't it!"

Helen blurted out, "you mean to tell us that you just looked at each other and formed a life time bond? I bet that doesn't happen very often. How serious were you two with your relationship?"

"We were very serious," I explained. "We were so much and so seriously in love from the very moment we met that we never ever in the least questioned our future. We felt that we were a couple like any married couple.

That is also the reason why the eleventh of November is so much more important to us than our actual wedding day. And I am not sure that our own kids are even aware of that date.

Something else we did that most couples don't seem to do, or at least not in such depth. We established rules that we would live by, rules that tackled anything from religion to disagreements. We defined what we meant by trust, fidelity, truthfulness, respect, and so on. Those rules and those definitions are as right for us today as they were in 1937, when we were teenagers. We have always lived by them and we have never encountered a serious problem in our life, for which we had not yet established rules.

Maybe one ingredient for a happy life, is to start early in life being mature, and then to retain your youth into your old age.

When Margo and I started to go together in 1937, Margo worked in downtown Berlin, while I was still in high school. There was not much time for the two of us to be together since my afternoons were filled also.

When I did not tutor students, I worked for one of our Math professors. This professor was writing the new German High School math book at that time. He had hired me to write the book's teacher edition, which contained the solutions to the new book's calculus problems. I also had to scrounge a few minutes a day for some of my homework. As you can see there was not much time left.

You may ask why I had to work while I was in High School. At that time High School was not free. High School, or 'Gymnasium', as it was called in German, had nothing in common with the American High School, except the name. It was strictly a preparation for the University. You did not choose subjects, it was a fixed curriculum. You didn't choose Latin, or French, or English.

At any rate, I had to pay twenty marks a month, and I had to buy my books. Then there was the fact that I wanted to have a little spending money, since Margo had just a few pennies of her own.

In the evening I worked as a projectionist at the local Movie Theater. That job required constant attention, since at that time we used arc lamps in the projection booth. They had to be adjusted almost constantly. And then, too, the film would break from time to time.

Not having much time together meant that whatever time was available was filled to the brim. In a big city, such as Berlin, privacy was difficult to come by during the day. But we found a somewhat seedy café. There, loving couples could have their coffee in a curtained booth, where the waiter would knock discretely before entering. We didn't care how seedy it was, we were in love, and here was privacy to hold hands and gaze into each other's eyes.

Whenever we did have time together in the evenings, we could be found in a city park just two blocks from where we lived. This was not as easy as it may sound today. My mother was doing everything in her power to keep us apart. To her mind, this girl Margo just was not a good enough catch for her only son, and she and I had many bitter arguments. Margo's stepmother, for reasons of her own, was also dead set against Margo and me being together. So, we always had to overcome many obstacles, by being sometimes devious and at other times rebellious.

But we did steal enough time to be together. Whenever I could, I would pick her up from work and we would walk home together, a whole hour of togetherness. Sometimes we would just sneak out the door. We knew full well that there would be many a heated word said later, but we learned to shrug them off.

# 9

After I graduated from High School there was even less time available, since I worked as a chemist at the German Bureau of Standards north of Berlin. My main job there was research into metal nitrides. It took me three months to work myself up to get my own laboratory assignment. What a position for a young guy without college education. But once given the opportunity I had shown that I could do the work.

I hated to leave there, but by law I had to join the compulsory 'Arbeitsdienst' in 1939. In the 'Arbeitsdienst' I worked for six months with a shovel and a spade in the eastern part of Germany. The 'Arbeitsdienst' was a 'Youth Labor Service' every young German had to join for at least a half a year.

After my shovel and spade interlude, I was hired as one of the seven chemists at the Auer Company in Berlin. There I had again my own laboratory. I prepared radioactive fillings for hollow core platinum needles, which I then soldered shut in a magnifying hood, using fine gold wire. Much easier was the preparation of platinum buttons, which I filled with radioactive material that I sintered in place.

My radioactive needles and buttons were used in radiation cancer therapy.

Let me digress at this point for a moment, because there is a little known story here.

The Auer Company where I worked, had the sole exploration rights for minerals at a mine near a small village named Joachimstal, in a region between Germany and Czechoslovakia. The tailings contained a fair amount of Uranium, Radium, Thorium etc. And from the tailings of this mine Madame Curie had obtained the radioactive materials she had used in her lab.

Later this mine also furnished the uranium for Prof. Otto Hahn and Lise Meitner, who were the first to split the atom in 1939, which naturally was the beginning of the atomic age. This mine had been in operation since the Middle Ages, at which time it was just a silver mine. From this silver they struck coins, which were called 'Joachimstaler'. Now this was too long a word even for the Germans, who are used to long words, and so they shortened the word and simply called the coins 'Taler'. And from this comes the word for our currency, the 'Dollar'.

Eddy slipped in a quick remark. "Whoa, that will come in handy the next time the guys and I play our freestyle version of Trivia Pursuit. That one will really stump them. Sorry for the interruption."

"No problem," I assured him.

"Now let's get back to Margo and me.

I never asked Margo if she would marry me, this was a foregone conclusion right from the start. And she didn't expect such a question, we were a couple and that was that.

The only friends we had were our mutual friend Hermann, and an older couple who lived in an apartment across the street from me. They lived together, although they were not married, and for that reason were shunned by everyone else. But they fully understood our free and rebellious spirit, being rebels themselves in a society, which did not condone 'living in sin'.

With them we sometimes spent a lively Saturday afternoon, being served coffee and German chocolate cake, talking about relationships, and canaries, and religion, and squirmy puppy dogs, and whatever else came to mind.

The reason for not having many friends was simply that we were non-conformists, and we were not afraid to show it openly. But this had one advantage. We were forced to discuss between ourselves how we were going to structure our lives, and what kind of ethics our relationship was to be based on. Many times later on in life we came across situations, which could have caused bitter arguments. And at those times we were glad that we had decided early on, how we would handle such problems.

We sometimes even stole away in the evening to visit a favorite haunt of ours, a wine pub called 'Uncle Bruno's'. It was located downtown and to enter you had to walk down about seven or eight steps, since it was located almost at basement level. We would sit in a booth of dark stained wood, festooned with fake ivy, which lent just enough color to the place to give it a very inviting and friendly atmosphere.

It did not take long before Uncle Bruno and we became fast friends and he often sat with us when business was slow. This friendship also meant that our meager financial resources stretched much further. I remember him fondly; Uncle Bruno showed a lot of generosity toward us. I think he probably enjoyed those two crazy lovebirds.

I recall one particular evening when Uncle Bruno informed us that he had just received a shipment of Greek wine. It came from the island of Samos and we were to be the first to taste the wine. Naturally, that wine was way beyond our meager means. But Uncle Bruno knew that, and so he told us that this night would be on him. The wine was heavy, it was sweet, and it had a powerful punch. We drank, we sang, and we had a wonderful time till early in the morning, when even Uncle Bruno had had enough wine.

And so it was fairly early in the morning when we left Uncle Bruno's wine cellar. We started home, still singing and in the best of spirits. I seem to remember that on the way home, we happily waved at the few pedestrians we met, who were walking to work early.

Now here I must digress again and explain how Margo could sneak into the house and into her apartment. Her parents, naturally, would not let her have a house or apartment key. However, one day she had had access to her father's keys and I hastily had made impressions of them in a new bar of soap. From them I could file a duplicate house key and an apartment key for her. That solved problem number one.

The second obstacle was a chain that her parents had installed inside their apartment door. But even this did not do the trick for them, Margo's wrists were small enough for her to just barely reach in and slowly move the chain out of the way. And so her parents never knew when she came home or how she managed to get in.

I believe that Margo's father knew more about our shenanigans than we realized at the time. And I cannot help but think, that he often understood, and felt with us, even though he could not openly condone our rebelliousness. Maybe secretly he even marveled at how we managed our life, despite the constant attempts of our mothers to stop our love affair.

One particular morning we went home later than usual, or shall I say earlier. I cannot say how long it took us to get to where we lived, but I do remember that the sun was trying to peek over the horizon, and that it was definitely getting light. After I had walked Margo home, I went home also.

I had only to walk the distance of about two blocks to my apartment, and I do recall being able to open the apartment house door. But I could not find the keyhole of the door to our apartment. I was really getting frustrated.

My mother finally awoke from the racket I must have been making and let me in. I also remember that I splashed cold water in my face, grabbed my school satchel, and hurried to catch my streetcar so I wouldn't be late for school.

When my mother let me in I apologized to her for the noises I had made, trying to find the keyhole. But I can't remember what my mother's answer was that night, only that it was not very friendly or understanding, when I explained to her what the problem had been. I guess she didn't believe me when I told her that someone during the night had stolen the keyhole."

I stopped here to let the laughter die down.

"I am glad you two didn't become winos because I wouldn't talk to you if you were," said Helen. "But how come Uncle Bruno let you into his place and even served you wine when you were still under age. At sixteen and seventeen you were still considered children and he should never have done that. The law is quite explicit about that."

I addressed her directly. "Remember, I told you that these were different times, we already were working, and we certainly did not act or feel like kids. We were aware of our responsibilities and would never have thought to hide behind the shield we apply today, when it is more important to feel good about yourself than be a responsible being.

But most of all, you have to stop trying to apply your US yardstick of today to a situation, which cannot be measured by that yardstick. Just as the people of that time would be appalled that nowadays you cannot spank your own kid for misdeeds without the danger of finding yourself in court.

You see, I am telling you my stories for two reasons. I want you to see what the times where like that we encountered. But I also try to tell stories that make you chuckle, like the one I just told you."

# 10

Now Eddy turned to me with a frown on his face.

"There is something that really puzzles me, Horst. How could Hitler get away with what he did. I mean, how did the Germans really feel about him? Anyway, how was living under Hitler? Or maybe you don't want to talk about him, I won't blame you."

"So, you would like to hear about that part of history?" I asked him. "You understand that we can only tell you how we as young eye witnesses saw the Hitler regime."

Yes, he and the others agreed, they would like to have us tell about Hitler, after all, this was one of the most vexing problems: How could Hitler manage so easily to take over, and so easily dupe an entire nation.

As you know there was a worldwide, deep depression in the early 1930s. In Germany one third of the people were unemployed. The existing democracy, the old Weimar Republic, was powerless to turn the economy around.

In the minds of most Germans there existed only two choices, international socialism, which means communism, or National Socialism. Both factions were equally strong, but Adolf Hitler's National Socialism appeared less threatening to most people than communism, which carried with it the real threat of Germany becoming a Russian satellite.

So Hitler was appointed in 1933, and it was not long after his appointment that Hitler was able, under a pretext, to outlaw the only real threat to his rule, the Communist Party. This then gave him an absolute majority in the German Parliament, which quickly enacted a law, the 'Empowerment Act', giving Hitler practically unlimited power. This he needed, it was said, to get the economy going again. From then on he legally could pass any law he wanted.

Many things Hitler did in 1933 and in 1934 looked very good to the public at the time. He commissioned Dr. Porsche to design a car that the average person would be able to afford, the VW or People's Car. When you signed up for a VW you were given a little booklet for stamps you bought every week.

And every week you could glue one stamp into your little book. When completely filled, it could be traded for a VW, which cost just shy of one thousand Marks, about 250 Dollars at the official exchange rate then. The first books were filled just at the outbreak of the war, in 1939. The Germans had financed a tidy factory for Adolf Hitler.

Nice timing, wasn't it?

And since there soon would be so many people with cars, so Hitler said, Germany needed a major network of automobile roads. Construction was started on this monumental task right away, putting millions to work building the Autobahn, four lane roads on which mechanized troops later could easily and speedily be moved about.

Nice coincidence, wasn't it?

With so many Germans now working hard they should also have entertainment, Hitler said. And so the People's Radio was born. Radios at that time were very expensive and few people could afford one, but this new radio was cheap, about $8.00. Naturally, it could receive only the local stations.

Nice of Hitler to give us a radio, right?

Now Hitler's propaganda machine was in every household. And, since the radio system in Germany always had been a government monopoly, it should not be a surprise that the news now was being managed by the Party.

The Romans coined a phrase, a recipe for ruling the people: 'Panem et Circenses'. Just give them bread and entertainment and they will be happy. Hitler knew that, he gave the Germans a chance to work and make a decent living, and he made sure there was entertainment.

In Berlin there were over fifteen opera houses and theaters, and for the small price of one Mark, which was 25 cents, one bought a ticket, then reached into a revolving drum to get one's seat assignment, kind of a lottery. We were always lucky and had some of the best seats in the house, because Margo picked the final ticket.

Everything looked great on the surface in 1934, the economy was moving and people had work. Cruise ships were under construction to take workers on holidays to the Azores and other exotic places. National pride was soaring, and hopes were rekindled that the German territories lost after WW One might return.

One of the biggest historical blunders ever had been the carving away of many German territories after WW One. They had then been given to the neighboring countries. Now many Germans lived under foreign flags. National sentiment and feelings were much stronger in Europe at that time than today, and Hitler knew how to fan the nationalistic flames.

The Saar Region, where I had spent my early youth, was very rich in coal. It had been eyed as a prize by France, who had occupied the region at the end of WW One, in 1918. Then, 17 years later, in 1935, a plebiscite was finally held under international control. I seem to remember that the results were better than 95% in favor of a return to Germany. But this was the only region where people had had a chance to voice their opinions regarding their national affiliation.

Another huge blunder was the continued occupation of the Rhineland. The Rhine River in the heart of Germans always has been an almost sacred place. Having it occupied by foreign troops for almost twenty years after the end of the war was a festering sore and an insult to the national pride.

I always thought that it had been a stupid decision by the Allies to do that. They even cut Germany in half by giving the so-called Polish Corridor to Poland. There surely were other ways to let Poland have an access to the Baltic Sea.

# 11

There was also a national plebiscite in Germany in 1934 and it turned out that the vast majority of Germans were definitely pro Hitler then. The war was still years away. At that time many of Hitler's speeches started with, 'I was a soldier during the last war and I know the horrors of war. There will never be another war.'

Yes, he also talked about the Arian race being superior, and about how the Jews were trying to undermine the new order. That Jews were leeches and parasites, all you had to do was look around you, he said. You will see Jews in all leading positions in Finance, Politics, Arts etc. Removing Jews from their influential positions was therefore one of his first acts, causing hundreds of thousands of Jews to leave the country. It was huge brain drain.

Hitler's and Stalin's regimes were fairly similar in many respects, except that Hitler, unlike Stalin, did not propose to nationalize every industry, every business, and every farm. There was still plenty of opportunity for the individual, and you still had a fair degree of personal freedom, unless you openly opposed the regime.

You could even make jokes about Göring or Göbbels without being thrown in jail. And while Hitler often raved against Capitalism, he still wanted Capitalism's competitive spirit in commerce and especially in science.

As long as you did not openly criticize or oppose the regime, you had little to fear. Just march in all parades as asked by the now nationalized unions and they left you alone.

The Nazis established special facilities, called concentration camps, where those went who could not keep their mouth shut. To make these camps appear somewhat legitimate to the public, the courts also sentenced people such as black marketers, people who embezzled public funds, etc., to these camps.

The prisoners returned from their experience a new person, with mouth shut tight, toeing the line. What went on behind the barbed wire of the concentration camps nobody seemed to know. At least no one talked about it, least of all those who returned.

Neither in Russia, nor in Germany, did the general population live in constant fear for one's life or liberty. You just had to be very careful and not make any waves; that could have had dire consequences.

I remember when we, that is our friend Hermann, Margo, and I, somehow latched on to an American jazz record, 'Tiger Rag'. This was before the war, about 1938. But before playing it on the record player, we carefully hung heavy blankets over the door and over the window to muffle the sound. Jazz was considered decadent music by the Nazis."

"You must be kidding," chimed in Helen, "how could music be a danger to a government. And also, what could they have possibly done to you, unless there was a law against playing jazz."

I turned to Helen. "Dear Helen, you have a lot to learn about living under a totalitarian system. And it matters not a bit, whether they are of the left variety, or the rightist kind, or even of the religious stripe. In fact the latter can easily be the worst.

In America we would have needed a law, but in a totalitarian system you don't need laws.

The Nazis probably would not have done much to us personally, but our parents soon may have been out of a job, or be transferred to the middle of a swamp. Or a number of other unpleasant things could have happened. No, you had to be careful.

But let me get on and talk a bit about the feared 'SS'.

It had always been the established doctrine of the Communist Party to be physically aggressive, kowtowing the opposition into silence. As history has shown after WW II, this also was the tactic of the Soviets in a number of Eastern countries. And so it was in Germany, where the Communist Party's main rival was Hitler's NSDAP, or National Socialist German Workers Party, the Nazis.

The Communist goons showed up at every NSDAP rally and tried physically to disrupt the proceedings, while at the same time intimidating the people to keep them from listening to the speeches of their archrival.

The NSDAP answered these tactics by creating a select cadre of dedicated party members, who were willing to protect the speakers, often a dangerous assignment. They wore black shirts and were called 'Saal Schutz', 'Premises Protection'. This name was later changed to 'Schutz Staffel', 'Protection Brigade'. But the initials stayed the same, 'SS'.

Out of this cadre of dedicated party members was later on recruited a bunch of fanatics who served under Himmler. From these ranks came the secret police. These fanatics were also the ruthless 'SS' goons, who later were responsible for the atrocities during the war. They were the feared guards at the concentration camps. And toward the latter part of the war, they were the responsible agents of the holocaust.

Most of the original 'SS', the idealists, by that time had long since left the 'SS' in disgust.

The name 'SS' was also given to certain military units, called the 'Waffen SS', who had distinguished themselves in battle, sort of an honorary title. The poor guys who had been drafted into those units suffered greatly later on, because no one made a distinction between 'SS' and 'Waffen SS'.

So there were actually three different units called 'SS', the idealists of the twenties and early thirties, the henchmen of the system, and the poor guys of the military units.

We must also stress that what we call the holocaust, the killing of millions of our Jewish population, did not start until late during the war. It may sound unbelievable that hardly anyone in Germany was aware that this was going on, but there are reasons for that.

We have often been told that we certainly must have known about it, when several million of our population were killed in extermination camps. The answer is simple. The extermination camps were located in Poland, close to the Russian border. The guards did not talk, no one came back from the camps to talk, and last but not least, it was a totalitarian system.

Even in an open society, such as in the US, a Manhattan project could employ thousands of people, and no one knew about it. The US even exploded the first A-bomb, and only a very few people in the country were aware of the fact that an A-bomb had been exploded on US soil.

Even the Western Allies were shocked at the end of the war, when they found out the extent of Hitler's atrocities. Just as no one knew the full extent of Stalin's atrocities. He had killed between 20 and 25 million people and very few knew of this. At least no one talked about it, neither in Russia, nor in the United States.

Even today, many Russians are unwilling to believe that this had happened almost under their noses so to speak, without them knowing. Just as many Germans today will still insist that it could not have happened in Germany.

But think about it, how can the news about such atrocities become known to the population in a strict totalitarian system. Under such a system all news comes from the government, the very organization that wants to keep these facts a secret. Global communication, such as satellites or the Internet, had not been invented yet. A few intrepid souls with the right radio could listen to the BBC. And they were very careful, this was a lot worse than listening to 'Tiger Rag'.

Let's assume you were a German, or a Russian, and you had known about these atrocities, would you have talked about them? Chances were good that you would have wound up in such a camp yourself if you talked.

The danger for us here is that people in the US are trying to measure other non-democratic systems and cultures with their US yardsticks. Just as Helen was doing a little while ago when we talked about Uncle Bruno's wine cellar.

I realize that you have no other yardstick. I fully understand the difficulty that people have, who have not experienced a totalitarian system first hand. With our Russian friends we don't have that problem, they and we have been there. And we understand when they tell about their times during the Soviet era, as they understand our situation.

The next time we get together I will tell you a bunch of Russian jokes and jokes from the Communist East Germany. Jokes are funny. But behind those jokes lurks a lot of truth, they are the only way to make statements without openly criticizing the government. And I think you will be able to sense what is behind them. It will be a good education for you.

OK, this then was what we saw and experienced. Naturally it cannot be a complete picture. After all, we were young and we had other things on our mind instead of affairs of state. And as other young people in other societies, we lived our lives basically untouched by politics."

# 12

# THE WAR YEARS

It was time to change the subject.

"Let's turn away from that unsavory part of history and be personal again," I told them.

But Bill had one more question. He turned to me, doing one of his fancy hand wavings towards no one in particular. "OK, that was a very good explanation but I still have one question. How come you guys fought so hard as soldiers when it became so obvious toward the end of the war that the war was lost?"

This question could have been posed to most any soldier ever, I thought to myself. Roman centurions, Napoleon's troops, Indian American tribes, and so on. But how could I explain that to my friends, who had never carried a rifle. I didn't think I could make them understand. But I tried anyway.

"If you are a soldier it just does not cross your mind just to throw away your weapon, unless you are cornered by the enemy and there is no way out. You probably are part of a platoon. And that is almost like a family. There are strong bonds and you just don't abandon your buddies. Getting the platoon together to talk about surrender will not do either. I guess you have to be a soldier to understand.

There is one more misconception. Once the allies were inside France, the average German soldier had had enough of war, and was looking forward to going home. There was no more fierce fighting, except by a few diehards. That's why the Allies swept across Germany like an express train. Now let's get personal again.

I for my part was never meant to be a soldier, despite of what my mother tried to drill into me. And how often did I hear her tell me about the family's great military tradition. Her side of the family, naturally. It was always the same, 'just look back at history,' the story started – 'was there not THE General Laudon who fought valiantly in the Balkans.' I always wondered though, did he do the fighting or did his troops?

I just did not have a great desire to enter the military, my dream for the future was chemistry. But there was little that could be done in 1940 but join the military before they drafted me, because by volunteering, I could at least choose the branch of the services. And that was why I found myself in basic training on an Air Force Base in a godforsaken place east of Berlin.

There we lived in hastily constructed wooden barracks, furnished with double stack bunks, twenty-four men to a building. The plumbing was located at one end of the compound and consisted of a long trough, above which ran a water pipe with faucets. There were no recreation facilities.

Instead we had a huge parade ground where drill sergeants tried to change us civilians into fighting men. My memories of this place are not of the most pleasant nature, but even so, there were some moments worth recounting.

One such occurred right at the start one day when the whole company was lined up for inspection outside the barracks. It was, I think, underwear inspection. At any rate, as the inspecting officer came to my pile I was supposed to give my rank, name, and serial number, which I did. It seems, however, that I did not announce myself loud enough, or forceful enough.

'Do you see the gate on the other side of the parade grounds', the lieutenant barked at me, and I answered, 'yes, Sir'.

'Get your ass over there, and I want to hear your rank, name, and serial number.'

I gave it my best and hollered as loud as I could, but all I received for my efforts was 'I still can't hear you, talk louder.'

When he finally had enough he shouted: 'Alright, soldier, get back here.'

I also had had enough and shouted back at him, 'beg your pardon, Sir, I couldn't hear you.'

That evening somebody must have signed in sick, because the Air Force was one person short for guard duty. It came as no great surprise to me that I was elected to be the replacement. That meant no sleep for another twenty-four hours. And tired as I was from a ten-hour parade drill, I reported for duty.

That night, as I made my rounds of the compound to keep my comrades safe from the enemy 2000 miles away, I came upon a door, which was slightly ajar. Now everybody knows that military doors must be kept closed at all times, and I had no choice but to investigate. Let me explain that this particular door was at one end of a barracks, which we had dubbed the ten-seater, in other words, it was the latrine.

When I arrived at the non-regulation door I opened it further to look in. I was at once greeted by an angry drill lieutenant who swore at me, 'close that door you imbecile', or something to that effect. But for once I rose to the occasion and became a model soldier.

'Yes, Sir,' I replied, 'but first I will have to report to you as my superior officer according to section 738 slash six,' or at least a similar silly number. And this said, I presented arms, again according to regulation, and started my litany of name, rank, serial number, password, etc, etc. After I finished I shouldered my carbine while the lieutenant meekly asked me to kindly close the door and let him have some privacy.

I did not see this drill lieutenant again until the afternoon the next day. I was standing in front of the telephone booth size guardhouse, the type that looks so pretty on postcards. Suddenly, the company commander appeared on my right with my beloved drill lieutenant in tow. Now I must confess that I had been somewhat inventive that afternoon, since it was a very hot day and I was standing guard in the full sun.

As was the custom at the time, a military guard had to not just be dressed in a most uncomfortable, hot uniform, which was buttoned to the neck. He had to add a bayonet to his shouldered carbine, which added still more weight to this stupid, and solely ceremonial, piece of equipment.

This day, however, I had had an inspiration. The guardhouse was built of wooden planks, which had shrunk over time. There was a crack between two planks right behind me, tailor-made for a bayonet tip to wedge between. All that remained was taking careful aim, imbed the tip of the bayonet, and the carbine was practically weightless. The sun by this time had moved behind me and when I suddenly heard the commander's footsteps I frantically pulled on the carbine to release the bayonet from its prison. I was fortunate to manage it in time, come to attention, and present arms while looking straight ahead.

But out of the corner of my eye I could see the commander hesitating a moment as he contemplated the fact that the guardhouse was rocking back and forth while the guard stood motionless a half a foot in front of it.

The lieutenant just gave me a somewhat quizzical glance but never mentioned the incident. But it seemed to reinforce his conviction that I needed special attention, and this he willingly did give me throughout the entire basic training.

I never had to volunteer, he saw to it that I received more than my fair share of any unpleasant duty. I don't believe he was very fond of me, and I can only say that I returned the feeling. But it is said that all is well that ends well.

The last time I saw the drill lieutenant he had a rather red face, as if he had rubbed it raw with brimstone. He never told us what had happened to his face, but I have it from a source close to me and unimpeachable that he had come home late the evening before we were to be shipped out.

Maybe he had had a few drinks celebrating my departure. At any rate, he had not turned on the light due to the advanced hour. He then obviously had turned the doorknob to his room, maybe wiped some sweat from his face and then went to bed.

He never found out who had smeared black shoe polish on his doorknob. But he might have guessed.

So you see, I was not exactly a shining example of a feared German soldier, far from it. But the war lasted and lasted and they did advance my rank, till at the end of the war I was a staff sergeant.

However, at one time during my soldiering career I was made a captain. But how that happened is another story. If you want to hear it, you will have to remind me later."

# 13

Here I had to stop 'to wash my hands' as the well mannered gentleman would say, or, in the ladies' parlance, 'powder my nose'. At any rate. I had to retreat for a short while. When I returned I was told to 'tell us some about the war'. But I switched to something much more pleasant.

"OK," I agreed. "Here is a wartime story that you will like, I am sure.

It was the end of September 1943, but the days were still pleasant and warm and this day was no exception. The sun was shining bright and cheerful in the sky and the air felt almost like spring.

This I didn't know as yet, I was still soundly asleep. But not for long. The persistent ringing of the doorbell put an abrupt end to my peaceful slumber. And when I finally answered the door, I found my wife's thumb still pressed against the doorbell.

I must explain again that at that time Margo was my wife as far as I was concerned. That was how we perceived our relationship. The law's perception, however, was otherwise and therefore Margo and I had agreed to make our bond official.

She was now over 21 and could get married without anyone's permission. And this then was going to be that special day.

We had announced our intentions the year before, at Christmas 1942 to be exact. We had had cards printed and mailed that solemnly pronounced to the world that Horst and Margo had become engaged. This momentous decision came about because we had no Christmas gifts to give each other, which, I guess, is as good a reason as any. I don't mean to get engaged, but to announce the fact.

At that time I was in an Army field hospital in Poland with no chance to get a short pass to visit Margo in Berlin. But Margo was not to be deterred. She somehow finagled a permit for a train ticket and arrived in Poland to visit me on Christmas Eve to my great surprise and my even greater joy.

I even was allowed a pass out of the hospital for the evening so we could spend some time together.

To this day, I think that having those cards printed was one of the best gifts we ever gave each other. Although making this public announcement to our families and friends was really unnecessary. Everyone knew that we belonged together. After all, we had been quite open about being a couple for the last five years. Some even said, shamelessly open.

There was a slight problem, however. Gold wedding bands were out of the question, gold was not to be had at this time during the war. But we did find a ring, made of stainless steel, which we both liked. However, the jeweler had only one ring, and it was my size.

That was why Margo had to buy her own wedding ring later, after she had returned to Berlin. Come to think of it, I believe I never reimbursed her for the cost and now it is too late, the Statute of Limitations has run out.

That was a precedent, however. Because on this day in 1943, since I had almost overslept my wedding day, Margo had had to buy her own wedding bouquet that morning. At the time I could only hope that she wouldn't take this as an omen of what was to come.

Needless to say, I hurriedly shaved, splashed cold water in my face, combed my hair, and hopped into my freshly pressed Air Force uniform. I was barely in time to meet up with her father, who walked with us to the Tempelhof Airport.

From there we took the yellow Berlin streetcar to the Tempelhof City Hall and presented ourselves to the magistrate. Margo looked ravishing, I thought, in the pretty dress she had borrowed from her sister-in-law. But at least the black shoes were her own.

There was just one small obstacle to hurdle when we arrived. We needed a second witness for this momentous undertaking. Fortunately I saw a lone soldier walking past outside City Hall and cajoled him into joining us for 10 minutes. We never learned who he was, or where he lived, or his name.

And so fortified we ventured forth to say our vows, in a bare, austere office. The dust had barely settled from last night's bombing. The ceiling and the walls had lost quite a bit of plaster, but this in no way dampened our spirits. There were just the four of us, her father, my sweetheart, myself, and the stranger, an Army private.

It was a short and solemn affair with just one small exception. Let me explain.

Margo's middle initial stands for Eleonore, a name she stubbornly had kept a secret from me for a long time. Obviously, it was not a name to her liking. When she had finally broken down and told me her secret, I thought it was hilarious. And every so often I would call her 'Margo Eleonore', in jest naturally, such as when she had a good-natured ribbing coming, as in 'Margo Eleonore, behave yourself!'

One day I had told her that the magistrate would in all probability also call her 'Margo Eleonore' during the ceremony, and she better keep a straight face. And that was exactly what happened, he called her 'Margo Eleonore'. I stole a look at her, she glanced at me, and the serious ceremony almost erupted in uncontrolled laughter."

Here Eddy turned to his wife and said: "Hon, remind me never to get frivolous and call Margo by her middle name. I want to stay on good footing with her, and not miss out on her German cookies and cakes, they are too delicious."

# 14

"OK," I continued, "let's talk about cookies and cake and such. You understand that 1943 was the fourth year of war in Europe for us. Therefore I can only marvel at the ingenuity of Margo's stepmother. She somehow had been able to scrounge together enough materials to produce what easily passed as a wedding cake. It was proudly placed in the center of the big dining table in the dining room for all to admire.

After we returned from our simple wedding ceremony we sat down to some coffee first, leaving the cake for later. There were not too many guests that afternoon, just Margo's family, some close friends, and some of Margo's coworkers. I cannot remember all the wedding gifts, but two of them stand out in my memory. A set of three new wooden spoons for the kitchen that somebody had scared up somewhere.

And then came the prize of prizes, one shiny, brand new paring knife. How rich can you get! And what a change from then to today when brides expect a room full of expensive wedding gifts.

Margo's Dad broke open a bottle of good wine and everyone was having a wonderful time. Until the sirens started again and everybody hurried into the basement for a day raid. The bombs spared the building, but they fell close enough in front and in back, to shake and rattle not only our nerves but also the five-story structure. Chunks of plaster and brick were everywhere, when we crawled out of the basement, and we could well picture the damage on the fourth floor.

But what we grieved about most, as we trekked up the stairs after two hours, was the loss of the beautiful wedding cake, standing unprotected on the table upstairs. As expected, what greeted us as we entered the apartment, were chunks of ceiling plaster just everywhere we looked. But the bombs had not only let the plaster from the ceiling fall down, they had also dislodged the big dome shaped lampshade. And there the shade sat in the middle of the table like a giant turtle shell, protecting our wedding cake. We took it as a lucky omen.

I mentioned before that our parents were very much against our marriage, which was one reason we had to wait until after Margo's twenty-first birthday before we could apply for a marriage license. In 1942 I was still in Russia on the Leningrad (St Petersburg) front with no possibility of getting leave. So it was not until after I left the field hospital in Poland in January 1943 that we could set a date. I believe it was about June or July when I was granted a home leave by the Air Force for late September 1943. We still wondered what my mother's as well as Margo's stepmother's reactions would be.

As it turned out, Margo's father now had become our ally, and her stepmother, while not following his example, at least did not continue her open disapproval.

Horst Schneider

My mother at the time worked in what is now the Czech Republic, and while still dead set against our union, she had promised to be civilized and attend the wedding. She would arrive the day before our wedding, she wrote us. She even cabled us her train number and her arrival time, so we could meet her at the train station.

The train arrived on time. We scanned the arriving passengers, but my mother was not among them. That evening still we phoned her in Czecho-Slovakia. When we reached her landlady, where she had rented a room, the lady told us that my mother was not home at the moment.

Three days later, however, when we visited my mother, her landlady had a chance to talk to us in private and told us that she felt very bad about the answer she had given us when we had tried to reach my mother. She told us in strictest confidence that my mother was sitting not more than four feet from her when we had called. My mother even had told the landlady gleefully that her son would now have to call the wedding off, since his mother was not going to be in attendance.

But, as you already know, the wedding went ahead anyway.

# 15

Since my mother had not come to Berlin to attend our wedding, we became concerned and decided to take the train to visit her in Czechoslovakia. This train trip was part of why our married life started out a bit unusual. After a nice wedding day dinner we had had time for just one glass of wine before the air raid sirens started up again. So we had to spend most of our wedding night in the basement of Margo's father, listening to the unpleasant sounds outside.

At these times you always wondered if the building would collapse and you would be entombed, or maybe gassed if the gas line broke, or maybe drowned should the water lines break. Or you might be roasted, should you be trapped in a burning building. Our luck held and we laughed with relief. And then we decided to postpone our wedding night till that evening.

Naturally, being an unconventional couple, it wouldn't have been right to have a conventional wedding night. And conventional it certainly was not.

After the night raid was finally over we were too keyed up to sleep and had an early breakfast instead. And so fortified, we ventured to the train station to buy our tickets and be on our way to Czechoslovakia to find out what had happened to my mother.

It was late in the evening when we finally arrived at our destination, about 30 miles from where my mother lived. Since we could not travel farther that evening we had to stay and find a place for the night. But it was not to be; there was absolutely nothing available.

We whiled away most of the night in a bistro, sipping on some wine until closing time. The owner felt sorry for us and offered to let us stay in the back room, where we could at least sit in peace till morning. We accepted in a flash.

This particular room was a typical backroom of a bar, there were two old hat stands, some other assorted furniture, such as an old billiard table, and a bunch of chairs. And so it happened that this young and very tired couple spent their wedding night peacefully sleeping on a hard billiard table.

In retrospect I must say that that actually was the most pleasant part of our visit, compared to what followed. We knew we had to tell my mother that we had visited my father, and we dreaded it.

It had been the first time I met my father and he turned out to be a very kindhearted man. He had remarried, a young neighbor, the daughter of a greenhouse owner. He owned a house in the Odenwald, a mountain region east of Heidelberg. He had bought this house originally as a summerhouse. Later, after we had been bombed out in Berlin, in 1944, Margo lived there with him and his wife and fondly remembers the evenings, when my father played the old pump organ, his ever-present pipe between his teeth.

Having contacted my father was in my mother's eyes an unforgivable sin and the break between her and me became complete. My telling her of this contact was the last communication between her and us. Therefore she was unaware that we had immigrated to America or that she had become a grandmother.

It was a few years after we had arrived in America, when we lived in Colorado Springs, that Margo took the first step to an uneasy truce by writing her a letter. While the letter was not well received by my mother, because it had been Margo who wrote it, it still was a breakthrough. As Margo said, the time had come to be forgiving, mother was getting on in age and must be lonesome. And since somebody must take the first step, let it be us.

We realized that life had not been kind to her and we felt sorry for her. My father, as well as Margo's parents were well enough off and didn't need any assistance, but the old lady was alone and lonesome. We could not easily afford it, but we started to send her ten percent of our earnings every month to ease the last part of her life, and we are glad we did.

We even twice paid her airfare so she could visit us in Denver and see her grandkids and her great-grandkids. But twice was enough. She had mellowed somewhat over the years, although not enough to have her visit us a third time."

# 16

I wanted to get off that subject and turned to Bill. I asked him, "who of your two sons was it who was interested in aviation, especially in airplanes?" He didn't say a word but just pointed at Eddy. So I told Eddy, "I have a little story about aviation for you. It's a short story about some unusual airplanes." With that we settled down for a change of pace.

"In the late fall of 1943," I began, "I was stationed near Augsburg. I was at the time assigned to a heavy bomber wing. This particular bomber wing was being refitted with a brand new bomber, the Heinkel 177. That naturally meant a lot of pilot retraining.

This airplane was a very unusual design. It had two engines on each wing, each pair coupled together, turning one oversized prop. This arrangement brought the prop closer inboard, making the plane more maneuverable. The oversized prop also made the plane much quieter. The pilots who flew it on night raids over England liked it very much. I cannot remember ever having heard about a design similar to this one anywhere in the world. So maybe it was not such a good idea after all.

On this airfield were also stationed two other unusual designs, the first operational twin jet fighter, the Me 262, and the He 173, which we dubbed the Flying Egg. The latter looked somewhat like an egg with two stubby swept back wings. I believe someone told me that it was built out of something like plywood.

This plane was powered by a rocket engine burning exotic fuel. The pilot was lying prone inside. Looking at the plane I wondered if there was room inside for any more than the pilot. For takeoff it had a wheeled dolly, which the pilot jettisoned after takeoff, and for the landing it was equipped with a skid.

This plane was flown by a famous test pilot by the name of Hannah Reitch, the only German woman ever to be awarded the Iron Cross First Class. When Margo had visited me earlier in the year, she had had a chance to watch Hannah Reitch take off, which was a spectacular view since the plane went up almost vertically. Her test maneuvers were fun to watch, too. They looked like some choreographed dances.

I just mentioned that Margo had come to visit me for a week, for which I had secured a room in a neighboring village. And here I must take off my hat to Margo's father. When Margo had left Berlin she had asked her father to address any mail to her as Mrs. Schneider. Now this was before we were married and I am happy to say that her father did so.

While all this flying was going on I had plenty of time; there was no reconnaissance film to be developed or aerial pictures to be interpreted. So I found myself quite often riding my bike through the neighboring hamlets and villages, always ready with my camera.

Sometimes I took pictures of the farmers' kids, for which I was paid with cabbage, or potatoes, or even some bacon, whatever the farmer had, or was willing to part with. Such food was worth a King's Ransom at that time when there was very little food available in Germany. Naturally, I didn't take my pay immediately, but let it accumulate till I could get a pass and ride the train to Berlin.

I was lucky and got such a three-day pass to Berlin somewhere around late November of 1943, and at once collected my goodies to take with me. A big footlocker was requisitioned and packed on the day before I was to leave and this I left with one of the farmers since I couldn't possibly bring it onto the base.

When I left on Friday morning with my loot, the farmer helped me carry my footlocker to the local train station, which fortunately was not very far

First I had to take the local train to Augsburg. There I had to lug my 70-pound footlocker from one end of the station to the other. At least the train ride to Berlin was uneventful and we arrived at the outskirts when it was already pitch dark, about seven or eight. There the train stopped for a short while before very slowly proceeding into the city. It was about then that the usual circus started, the bombs were falling, the anti aircraft batteries went into full swing, while the train kept crawling along just a little faster than walking speed.

About four blocks west of where we lived was a deep depression, like a dry riverbed, in which ran about six rail lines leading into the city. That was the area we were slowly approaching. So it was only natural that I conceived the crazy idea to jump off the train at that point to be home in a few minutes.

Coconspirators were quickly found among some other soldiers. And as the train approached the overpass near our apartment, I jumped off the train. I then jogged next to it in the darkness, waiting for my buddies to throw the 70-pound footlocker on my back.

Looking back at this crazy venture I shudder. I must have survived, because I remember then crossing two empty rail tracks and two rail tracks with parked boxcars. But the embankment up to the street was much too steep for me with my burden and I had to leave the footlocker next to the last rail track.

After I had climbed over the six-foot wooden perimeter fence, I found that the main street was well lit indeed. One of the gas streetlights had been hit and the escaping gas had ignited. As I made my way home I found a soldier wandering around, looking for a way to get downtown to a train station.

The poor guy had been visiting his girl friend. But the air raid had started shortly after he had left her apartment, and in the dark, and then later, with fires burning around him, he was utterly lost and confused. I offered him a deal in return for his help with my loot that he couldn't refuse. Safe haven, a meal, a place to sleep and finally, in the morning, directions to his train station,

I cannot remember his name, but that is not important for this tale anyway. With his help we lifted the footlocker onto the top of the six-foot wooden fence where my new friend balanced it, while I climbed across to hold it from the other side.

After joining me, we triumphantly marched home just as the air raid was being cleared.

Margo had already returned from the basement when I rang the doorbell. It was quite an emotional greeting, since she hadn't known I was coming home for a weekend. She busied herself in the kitchen right away and before long the table was set for dinner in our little room, complete with a beautiful candle in the center.

'Congratulations,' mumbled my new buddy, while Margo was doing last minute things in the kitchen, 'you are a lucky man.'

'Yes,' I answered, 'I sure am a lucky guy to have such a sweet, loveable girl. And a wonderful figure to boot.'

'But not for long,' was his reply. 'Don't you know,' he explained when he saw my quizzical look, 'the lone candle on the table is a signal. It means she is pregnant.'

It was much later, when I could ask her if it was true that she was expecting. 'How did you know,' she answered in amazement, 'I was waiting to tell you when we were alone.'

It turned out she had not known about the significance of the candle, either. Setting a festive table was just her way of expressing her joy of seeing me.

# 17

But time marched on and finally, in 1944, it happened while Margo was in a bomb shelter. When she wanted to return home after the air raid she almost got lost, the landscape had changed so much. And all she could rescue of our belongings fitted into two suitcases.

Because of that I was given a three-day leave to relocate my family. We had already decided it was time to leave the city before we were bombed out, but I needed a three-day pass to do that.

My father had offered us to move in with him and his second wife in a house he owned, which he had used as a sort of summer resort. It was located in the mountains east of Heidelberg, in a small village called Unter-Schönmattenwag.

The locals pronounced this long name as Schimmeldewog. It was too long a name even to a German who, after all, is used to long words. And I will refer to it as Schimmeldewog also from here on. The official name is just too long. We knew that to get there we would be on the train all night and all day, and indeed, it did take that long.

When we left Berlin we could not get into the train

Horst Schneider

through the doors since the train was overcrowded with refugees, so we had to climb in through a window. Margo was pregnant in her fifth month and she had been without sleep for more than 48 hours when we arrived in Schimmeldewog. But here she was finally safe.

Let me tell you a bit about the period around 1943-45 in Berlin. This time was without question somewhat unusual, and it made for very unusual behavior at times. During that time you did not completely undress when you went to bed in the evening, because practically every night Berlin had an air raid.

The local radio shut down in the evening. So, instead of a program you heard only a ticking sound like an alarm clock. And when that ticking stopped you'd come fully awake, jump out of bed and get ready for another round of bombs falling.

Sometimes this early warning did not come in time and you awoke to bombs exploding and anti aircraft guns firing. That happened one night in 1944. Margo woke to the sound of explosions and anti aircraft fire and she was off her bed in a flash. She was about four months pregnant at the time and therefore had the special privilege to seek refuge in a huge concrete bomb shelter. This shelter had been built recently at the Tempelhof Airport, about six blocks away.

She also was allowed to be accompanied by one companion. That companion was her friend Maria who lived in the same house on the second floor. At the time Margo jumped off her bed Maria jumped off her toilet seat where she had been doing what one does there. And with her panties in her hand she came flying down the stairs.

What comes next may be hard to believe, but crazy times bring on crazy behavior.

The two young ladies started off at a fast jog toward the safety of the bomb shelter. They had run about three blocks when Maria suddenly stopped and said, 'I am not going any further. This is absolutely crazy. If they want to hit me they will and if not they won't.' And with that she plopped down on the curb. What else could Margo do but join her.

So that night, Margo and Maria were sitting side by side on the curb in the street. They watched the bombs crashing around them, the buildings around them burning, the bright searchlights stabbing into the sky. They talked and joked, waiting for the end of the air raid, while red hot flak shrapnel rained around them.

Luckily for me they were spared that night. Maybe it was St. Peter who intervened because he didn't want to have to greet two crazy young ladies at his door, one still holding her panties in her hand."

# 18

I stopped till they finished laughing and I thought to myself that I should break off here for tonight. And also, what I didn't say, I had had enough of war for a while. It's not exactly my favorite subject.

Helen could not hold back any longer. She turned to Margo and asked, "what were you thinking, sitting there. I mean, you could have been hit any moment, weren't you scared? I know I would probably have died of fright."

Margo sat quietly and thought for a moment or two before she answered. "You know, Helen, I don't think I can give you a real good answer, except that you don't act normally anymore after a while. Sitting here I now shudder myself. But at that time I just did it. This probably is not a good answer, but it's the best I can do."

"No more stories tonight," I announced and turned to my four visitors. "Now it's your turn till tomorrow." So we settled down and talked about other things while we had another glass of wine.

"We will leave you alone for tonight," they said, "but only if you promise to tell us some more of your story tomorrow."

I also had to promise we would join them for dinner tomorrow, Saturday. That meant that we would talk before dinner, which was OK with me.

# 19

I knew they were going to be on time today, which gave me a chance to prepare myself mentally, and also to have a bit of time to think of some stories they might want to hear.

"I think I know where I want to start today," I told them. "I know that I want to get the wartime behind me, unless you have a special request."

"Oh yes," Eddy answered. "You were telling us a yesterday that you had been a captain for a short time, and I was supposed to remind you of that story if the occasion ever came up."

"OK," I laughed. "As you know, I rather tell funny stories than serious ones. So here it is.

In the winter of 1943 the German Air Force sent me to an advanced course in photo interpretation, which was conducted just outside of Berlin. It was only natural that I spent every minute with Margo when I could get a pass off base. The problem here was the return trip from Berlin to the base. I had to take a train, which at that time of night ran only once an hour. Then I still had a half-hour walk in the snow through the woods.

We tried very hard to get to the station in time

so I wouldn't miss my train, but we were in love, we were young, we saw each other so infrequently, and it was hard to say good-bye. I was fairly safe from the air raids where I was stationed, but Margo had to go back to where the bombs rained every night.

It was no wonder then that on three occasions I missed my train to get me to the base on time. At that time I was a staff sergeant and I had to be back on base by midnight. On these three occasions, when I did not make the deadline, I still got in somehow.

We had an agreement in the barracks that a missing person's bed was prepared as if somebody was under the covers sleeping. So I was at least somewhat safe from being discovered by the officer on duty.

That left me with only the problem of how to get through the gate. The first time I did not go through the gate. I remembered that they had been working along the fence on the outside of the base and I was in luck.

Some of the heavy-duty equipment was still parked next to the fence when I got to the work area. It was easy to climb up the equipment and then jump over the fence. I just had to make sure to mingle my footprints with the traffic on the main road before going to my quarters. Nothing fancy about getting across this way. The other two instances were much more interesting.

The second time I was late I had to change my attack, the equipment I had used had been moved. I decided to bluff it out with the guard who was certainly of a low rank, was younger, had less experience, was maybe even a new recruit, and would be easily rattled. He certainly was tired after a day of duty, and he certainly was bored. So I was sure that I could bluff my way inside.

I approached the gate with a purposeful stride and rang the bell. The guard came out and opened the gate. I couldn't afford to let him see my sergeant stripes, so I stood sideways with one sleeve against a post, the other facing away from him.

The moment he swung the gate open I took two steps, moving close to his face. I looked him straight in the eye and addressed him in my best drill sergeant voice: 'Is this the best salute you can muster, soldier?'

I didn't wait for an answer and marched on to my barracks. This poor fellow never had a chance to see my insignia or check my pass. And I didn't even feel sorry for him.

Another time I missed my train I was in luck to meet an understanding captain. While walking through the woods we talked about many things. He had a desk job and naturally was very interested in my tour of duty in Russia. He told me of his family and I talked of my sweetheart in Berlin.

He was not yet married but had a girl waiting for him many miles away in Dresden. So he could easily understand why I missed my train and he offered me an unusual solution.

That night two captains entered the base, one carrying his coat over his arm, not wearing it, despite the cold and the snow. His companion, however, the other captain, was nice and warm in an overcoat. But as soon as they were out of sight of the guard they exchanged coats. And after a hearty handshake, a captain and a staff sergeant parted and went to their respective quarters. It was a short-lived promotion.

# 20

Now let me get that crazy war out of the way by telling you about my last day on the frontline.

The day was December 13, 1944. The place was somewhere just inside Germany, near the Belgian border. The time was early afternoon.

My soft Air Force life as a photo interpreter had come to an end. I had been transferred and now was a paratrooper, at least in name.

Our company was down to 16 guys, holed up in a two-story house next to a road. It was a typical German secondary road, flanked for miles by trees on both sides. Between the trees, along the road, foxholes had been dug, mainly as places of refuge against strafing enemy planes.

To the left of the house, when viewed from the front, stood a detached structure. It was meant perhaps as a future garage or a workshop. At the present it was just a shell of bricks with large square holes for future windows. Behind the house was a neat little garden.

There was nothing for us to do but wait for the evening until we could disappear into the countryside. The front had advanced to about four miles behind us and we were convinced that we could become civilians within hours and leave the war behind us.

I was outside near the garage when a tank appeared on the road and started to shoot at me. And as I jumped into the building the bullets came through the brick and whizzed around inside, red-hot and angry. The first line of bullets went over my head, but then they aimed a second row of bullets about two feet above the floor and I had to do a Tarzan routine, swinging from the rafters.

Meanwhile, one of the guys went to the front living room, grabbed a bazooka and blasted the tank. I think it also blasted his eardrums, poor fellow.

With this immediate threat gone I jumped down, collected my Tommy gun, and made my way back to the house.

It was not long after that incident that an artillery barrage started and everyone piled into the basement. After my capture I had to give up my belt and my jacket, leaving me with boots, socks, pants, shirt, and underpants.

That night, after I had been interrogated, I found myself standing in a courtyard, facing a brick wall, with my hands held high above my head. It seems to me that I stood there for endless hours, but it probably was only one or two.

The next day we were marched to a holding area in a soggy cattle pasture. My area was under about one inch of water. So it was impossible to lie down and sleep, no matter how exhausted I was. This then was my third night without sleep, since the night before our capture we had marched all night to get into position.

Fortunately, it was still balmy during the day, and only cold at night, but not cold enough yet to form more than just a hint of ice on the water in the meadow. But still I felt the cold at night bitterly. Not having eaten for a day, and not having a jacket to wear made for a very long night indeed.

In the morning we were marched to a place nearby where we were supposed to dig graves. But even the American GIs could see that we were in no condition to do any physical labor, and so they looked the other way. I spent one more night in that meadow without sleep, but then on the third day we were loaded into boxcars, sixty men to a boxcar.

We also were given real food, called K rations. Those were cans with pork and beans, or hash, etc. Each of us also received one specially marked can, which contained a mixture of things, such as a three-pack of cigarettes, a candy bar, and similar frill items.

My memory here is getting hazy, but I do recall that we feasted on the K rations in the dark. I do recall that the train was rolling and stopping and rolling again, seemingly all through the night. But later I found out that we did not go further than maybe 200 km at the most. When we were let out it was daylight, and we were somewhere in Belgium.

With sixty guys in the closed boxcar there had been only standing room. The air had been stale already in the beginning, but then it became almost intolerable as the night progressed. Many of the guys had become ill after finally eating some solid food. And since toilet facilities were not available, we had to designate one corner as the toilet area, pushing everyone together even closer.

This then was my fifth night without sleep, trying to stand up in the dark, stinking car, being jostled back and forth and sideways as the train moved, and stopped, and moved again. We didn't find out that two fellows had died during the night until the journey finally came to an end."

I stopped for a moment to clear my throat when Helen spoke up. "This is inhuman. How can any human endure something like that and not go crazy. You must have had bad nightmares for many years afterwards. I read about soldiers having those nightmares for a long time after a war. An experience like this must leave, like, some kind of scar on the brain or the psyche or somewhere."

"Dear Helen," I answered. "A war is never pretty, whichever side you are on. But human nature is much more resilient than you think. In situations like these you don't think, you don't pity yourself or anyone else. You just exist and try to do the best you can under the circumstances. When the present is like a huge mountain, the future is far, far away.

Yes, I had some nightmares after I came home from the war but not very often, I quickly laid all this aside as past history. I am a fellow who lives with gusto in the present, and some in the future. But not much in the past, except when I tell a story.

I also believe we humans are a motley bunch and we don't all react the same. Anyway, that's all down the drain and I'd rather put all that in the inactive file. So let's get on with it and finish it.

# 21

We just talked about how the human brain might react. Well, the human brain fortunately blocks out many unhappy details. Therefore I have only partial memories of what was happening around and with me until much later when I was on my way to the US.

So the time from December 1944, to about March 1945, is not like a movie, continuous, with just a few intermissions. It is rather like a scrapbook with snapshots, many of them torn, or faded, or entirely missing. A few snapshots that are left in the scrapbook I can describe for you.

I don't know in which city we were let out, but I do know that it was only a short march to a compound, which seemed to have been a factory under construction. And here I have a vivid, almost tangible, recollection of a bare concrete floor in a huge empty room with large rectangular openings in the wall for windows. I can still see and feel myself making a beeline for the far left corner and collapsing there. I had not slept for five nights. And how long I slept there I don't know. Only that I was given some warm porridge when I came to.

Next we were loaded onto trucks and driven to a former German airfield. There we set up big Army tents after we had scraped away an inch or so of snow with our bare hands.

There was no straw, no blankets, or any other ground cover, we just slept on the bare ground as close together as possible for body warmth. For food we had a few crackers and a spoonful of orange marmalade a day.

Luckily, the weather was good, and the sun was shining during the day. I can still see myself sitting in front of the tent, my shirt in my lap, feeling along the seams and cracking lice between the nails of my two thumbs.

I also see myself walking in line with other prisoners for two hours every day, round and round like horses in a circus ring. This we did daily, and in order to keep some semblance of sanity while stumbling along like a zombie, I was shaping a spoon from a piece of wood I had found. I shaped it by scraping it with the sharp edge of a piece of glass I had found also.

I must have been in this compound for about two months before I was transferred to another compound. There the prisoners had had access to tools and had dug their quarters into the ground, somewhat like a prehistoric pit house. We even started to get warm soup once a day. And after someone found a coat for me I was finally warm.

And it was here, in the spring of 1945, that I was led out to a US military barracks where they interrogated me. They wanted to know where I had worked as a chemist, what my specialty was, etc. A short time later they offered me a one-year contract to work in the US.

After the war I found out that this program was called 'Operation Paperclip, a program, which brought many German scientists temporarily to the US. Now here was an offer I could not refuse.

By now I had accumulated several riches, a sharp nail, a stub of a pencil, a razorblade, and a small fabric sack, which at one time had held Bull Durham cigarette tobacco. And then there was my wooden spoon. All these items, except the spoon, I had found at one time or another.

It was just a few days later that I found myself on a train to Marseilles where I and many other POWs were loaded into the holds of a Liberty Ship. This one was outfitted as a troop transport with row after row of hammock like beds, six high. The food was the same every day, a kind of soup consisting mostly of spinach, or so we thought it was.

The ship creaked and groaned, and when the swell grew a bit higher and lifted the bow out of the water, we were in for a treat. The bow of the ship would come down with a mighty bang, making the whole ship shudder and shake. Inside the holds it sounded as if the ship was breaking apart and the end was near.

Once during the trip to the US we were allowed on deck for a few minutes for a breath of fresh air and I thought that I could almost feel the presence of a German submarine lurking in the vicinity, ready to sink us."

"My neighbor Sam told me about those Liberty Ships," Eddy interjected. "Sam had to ride in one in the Pacific, he didn't like it either."

So it turned out that somewhere was a kindred soul who also had sweated it out in a Liberty Ship.

# 22

"We finally landed in Boston and were sent one by one to a room filled with desks, each staffed by a GI. There I was ordered to hand over all my worldly possessions, which were duly recorded before they disappeared into a cardboard box next to the desk. My heart sank as the only things I possessed were discarded right before my eyes, I was stripped naked, so to speak. It was an utterly horrible, helpless feeling, and even today, after all these years, I can still recall it. And it may sound silly today, but not then.

We were then sent through a hot, soapy shower, we were deloused, and finally emerged at the other end where we were given a clean towel, so we could dry ourselves. Then came a short physical inspection, and back we went to the desks to be given back our belongings. What joy, I again was the owner of a nail, a spoon, a pencil stub, a razor blade, and a Bull Durham tobacco sack.

After a while we were marched to waiting Pullman rail cars. Each POW had a whole bench to himself, and to make heaven complete, a POW in white appeared to offer sandwiches, plus the choice of a banana or an orange, neither of which we had seen in many years. And as I looked out the window into the harbor I could hardly believe my eyes. The trucks and all the other machinery, such as front-end loaders and forklifts, were driven and operated by women, all pretty with makeup and lipstick.

The change from the Belgian POW camp to Boston harbor, pretty women, sandwiches, and oranges was almost too much. But even greater wonders awaited us when we arrived in Colorado Springs, at Camp Carson, which today is Ft. Carson.

There was a large POW camp just outside the Army Base where I was to stay for several weeks. I was told that I was to be a member of a team of sixteen POWs. And this was the place where I had to wait for the arrival of the remainder of the team. I also found out that we sixteen were to work at the Naval Academy in Maryland.

As we entered the barracks to which we were assigned we found on each bed a toiletry package with soap, razor, comb, etc. This then really was heaven we concluded.

But it didn't stop there. We were called out for chow and there was a mess hall with neatly set long tables. A hot dinner was served with real coffee and a welcoming cake for each table. We danced and whooped and gorged ourselves.

Later that night, however, we had to pay the piper. We were not used to real food after so many months without proper food. As a result, one after the other of us turned green, our innards churned and twisted, and most of us had to give up not only the sweet and heavy cake, but all the rest we had enjoyed so much just two hours before.

Colorado Springs was also the place where I buckled down to learn American English in earnest. I set myself a goal of acquiring a minimum of twenty new words a day. Naturally, I never knew if the new words I learned were uncommon or common words. Luckily, the majority was usable because they came from newspapers, but some, like juxtaposition or ululation, caused quite a bit of head scratching among the GIs when I used them. And I did my head scratching when I tried to understand what I saw in the comics, such as 'gotta', 'gotcha', and similar words and phrases. There was much new English to learn, which my British School English had not taught me.

While there I even volunteered for work and was sent to Nebraska where we worked in the sugar beet fields, blocking and hoeing sugar beets. It was backbreaking labor and not at all to my liking. We had to get up before dawn and came home after dark, and I was glad when I was sent back to Camp Carson because several more of our team had arrived there.

But just staying in camp was boring and so I again looked for something to do. This time, when I volunteered, I was sent to work on the Army base as night fire stoker. As such I had to make the rounds of a number of barracks to make sure that the boilers and the furnaces were properly fed with coal, and I was to do the feeding.

It didn't take too long to find out the optimum way to shovel just the right amount of coal and to place the coal on the grates just right. And pretty soon I had plenty of time to socialize. By socializing I mean that in the morning I would wake the cook and help him set up breakfast, in exchange for eggs and pancakes, naturally.

I was also the local host, since I commanded a hidden, out of the way place where the GIs could celebrate their coming discharge or whatever long after curfew. That's how I soon came into the possession of a pocket flask, labeled VODKA, which I filled with plain water. The next morning as I walked through the gate after work I was stopped immediately as I had anticipated. 'Whatcha got in that bottle?' asked the guard, and I replied: 'Vodka.'

'Open it,' was the next command. This I did, handing the guard the bottle. He sniffed, handed it back to me, and waived me on.

This charade we did maybe three or four times, after which he would wave me through without a further look. And that was how one POW in this camp was very popular, being the only one to dole out liquor to his friends.

Now I will admit that it was not exactly a great vacation being a POW, but in my case at least, I now had a damn good life.

There was just one big problem. I was worried about the safety of Margo and my child. I didn't even know if was a boy or a girl. And there was no way to find out anything, and that uncertainty was always nagging in the background.

So now let me switch for a while to Margo and her stories. "Or would you rather tell your own, dear," I asked her.

"Oh no," was her answer, "you are the storyteller, you are good at it, so let me just sit here and work on my knitting."

# 23

While I was a POW, Margo lived in the small village of Schimmeldewog in my father's house, where she had gone after we had been bombed out in Berlin.

At the north end of the village was a narrow one-lane gravel road that branched off the main road to the west. It crossed a creek, swung past the old mill, and then turned south to run steeply uphill past her house. At the south end of Dad's property the road branched again. The main branch turned west past some fields, then past the forester's mansion, turning into just a logging road, and finally it ran up into the forest as a trail. Further on it ran across a small mountain pass, which I had to cross a few times when I later worked in Stuttgart.

I just mentioned a mill by the road. That mill was still working in 1945, just as in the old days. Inside were two huge round millstones where they ground rye and wheat. The whole affair was driven by an ancient waterwheel, which was fed by the creek. That was the mill where Margo baked her weekly sourdough-and-potato bread, which she prepared at home and then carried down to the mill for baking.

It was up this steep, narrow gravel road that a noisy US Army tank rumbled toward the house at the end of the war. And this was Margo's first encounter with the US Army. The tank took up a menacing position between the neighboring house and Margo's. From there it had a clear and commanding view of the village. It was a frightening experience for her.

Her next encounter was with a GI who came to check the houses for weapons. He spoke some German and commented on a photo of me he saw standing on the dresser. He wanted to know my whereabouts, which Margo did not know, except that I had been on the western front.

Margo was quite frightened since the German propaganda had claimed that the Allies would take all German children away from their parents for re-education. But this GI seemed so concerned and understanding that she lost some of her fear. And she was really amazed when he tried to comfort her by saying that I was probably in good hands if I had been captured by US Forces.

The next visit by US soldiers started to calm her even more. They were looking for a house to use as their headquarters. They told her that her house was the best for the purpose, and also that it was situated best strategically. Then they told her they wouldn't consider it for their HQ since they did not want to displace so many people. They selected a house two doors north of Margo's, whose inhabitants had relatives in the village, causing less of a hardship.

Her attitude really changed when another soldier came later to string communication wires through the garden. He practically apologized for invading her property and promised to be very careful not to damage anything.

But the final chapter happened later in the year. Our daughter Sigrid contracted typhoid fever and was on the verge of death. She and Margo had been quarantined in the upstairs room, which faced out to our neighbors to the north. Sigrid had lost so much weight, she was unable so sit up; she was even too weak to lift a spoon.

The local doctor had told Margo that Sigrid could only be fed rice and raw grated apples, and should have only black tea as liquid, this at a time when rice or black tea had not been seen in Germany for years.

But just when there was no more hope left a miracle happened. A big bag with rice and a package of black tea appeared one day at the doorstep. There was no note attached, but everyone knew that only the US troops had rice and tea. Had the good doctor dropped a hint to the occupation forces? Margo never found out. But I know that it was Sigrid's future countrymen who saved her life.

# 24

Toward the end of World War II the Hitler government drafted even sixteen-year olds for all sorts of military duty, even manning anti aircraft guns. And that was how Margo's brother Erwin found himself suddenly in uniform. And as fate would have it, he was taken prisoner and sent to a POW camp in Mannheim where he was given duties in a US Army Supply Depot.

He was somehow able to get word to Margo about where he was located and Margo promptly made her way to Mannheim to visit him. It is true that most POWs as well as practically all civilians had a tough time because there just was not enough food to go around, but the fellows in the US Supply Depot did not miss much besides their freedom.

The German money at that time had lost its value since there was no merchandise you could buy, everything was in extremely short supply, or rather not available at all. To get soap, glass, extra food, shoes, or even nails, you had to barter. The standard currency was American cigarettes, or bars of soap, or ladies nylons. And the only source for those items was the US Army. A pack of Camels or Chesterfields was equal in value to a week's wages.

The US Supply Depot was therefore a gold mine for anyone working there, and both the Gis, as well as the German POWs, were forever inventing new schemes to smuggle merchandise out of the depot. Many a pair of nylons rode out of the depot in official US vehicles in tire tubes that had been cut open, filled, repaired, and reinstalled.

When Margo visited her brother in the POW camp she was appalled to notice that the white markings on the Army football field were not made with chalk but with precious rice. There was plenty of rice available in the supply depot but it was completely unavailable outside.

And that was not the only food item that the POWs of Erwin's camp could easily get. Erwin and his friends had not had any outside contact until then and were completely unaware of the situation in the city. Needless to say they asked her to come back a week later so they could gather as much food as they could.

This was in early December of 1945, and the journey from where Margo lived in the mountains east of Heidelberg was an affair of almost a whole day. First she had to walk about 6 miles to the next town, then walk a few miles across a divide.

The war had just ended, there were no sand trucks or snowplows to clear the road. And to make matters worse, the railroad tunnel connecting the two sides of the divide, had been dynamited by the retreating German troops. That meant one had to travel on foot over the divide to get to the rail station on the other side.

So she put on another, heavier pair of socks over her shoes to help her walk on the ice, and started hiking through the snow on the icy road.

Once on the other side she could pick up the train, then make a train change in the next city, which took her to Mannheim. She would have done this trek, and back again in the evening, in the dark, for just a half pound of rice. But the POWs at the camp had gathered so much more than that, enough in fact, to fill a whole suitcase.

There remained two problems. First, how to get the food out of the POW camp past the US military guard. He had inspected Margo's empty suitcase when she arrived but now it was full. And then there was the problem how to get the filled suitcase home without being stopped and searched on the way.

Getting past the guard turned out to be fairly easy. The POWs distracted him, while Margo walked past pretending to swing an empty suitcase. But on her way to the railway station she had to duck into quite a number of apartment house entrances whenever a patrol appeared.

This was her one and only food trip to her brother's POW camp, since just a few days later she slipped on some ice in the village and broke the ankle of her right foot."

"I can't believe the Army used rice for football field markings when people were almost dying because of lack of food. How cruel," Helen burst out.

"Let me put this in perspective," I explained to her. "The soldiers didn't either know how desperate the food situation was for the Germans. It was still almost war, Germans were the enemy, and there were many pressing issues for the Occupation Forces. At

any rate, one cannot measure using today's ruler. I
don't know how to explain the situation any better.
I guess one has to have lived through some crazy
times like those to understand them.

So there were no more forays to Mannheim
for her. But it was fortunate that the local doctor
owned a car. And it was even more fortunate that
he still had some gasoline. He had enough anyway
to drive Margo to the hospital where the bones were
set. Unfortunately it was done not only very poorly,
it was done incorrectly. There were hardly any
physicians left at home, most had been drafted and
were now POWs. Hospitals did the best they could
with whatever manpower they had.

It was also fortunate that this happened during
the winter because the summer and fall times were
busy times. Berries had to be picked in the woods,
while whistling or singing all the time, or making
other noises, to keep the wild boars away. But these
berries were not for food for her kitchen, they were
strictly for barter with farmers further to the north.

# 25

Every so often she would mount her bike and pedal twenty or so miles to an area where there lived some more prosperous farmers. There she would peddle her berries and mushrooms for any food she could get. In the afternoon she would then make the return trip, maybe with some bacon, or some flour, or some potatoes in a sack on the handlebar. The return trip fortunately was a bit easier because it was downhill.

Summer was also the time when wood had to be cut high on the mountain. The forest warden would assign a certain area, and all dead trees and branches, down to the thickness of a finger, had to be cut to the length of one meter and carried to the nearest road. There it had to be stacked according to type of wood and according to thickness.

And Margo was the only young and able-bodied person in the household of seven elderly people to hike into the mountains and be the lumberjack, cutting, sawing, stacking, and hauling the wood.

Gas or coal was unobtainable, and electricity was rationed to two hours per day, but you never knew when this would happen. Those two hours could be anytime during the day or the night. In the evening they used kerosene lanterns unless electricity was available.

That meant that all cooking, laundering, as well as heating, was done with wood. The forester who had assigned the area also marked those trees that had to be felled and stacked. He would measure the wood stacks and write out the bill. Margo then would hire a farmer with a team of oxen to bring the wood down the mountain.

There was just one more chore connected with the whole affair. It was not the farmer who loaded the wood and later     unloaded it. That was Margo's job also. And don't get the idea that the wood was free, the government charged heavy for it. After the wood was finally home, came the chore of sawing it to size, splitting it, and setting it up outside the house.

It was much later, after I returned home from America, that I learned more about her lumberjack ventures. When Margo and I together hiked up into the mountains, the first time after my return, to cut the wood, I learned how well she handled her axe and the big saws. I was mighty impressed, and then I was impressed even more, when I found out that she had gone out getting wood in the mountains even in 1944, when she was eight months pregnant.

Outside the house, a few steps away from the house, was a long trough, hewn out of a block of sandstone. The water faucet at one end was connected to a natural spring further up the mountainside. But during the winter the water tap froze and the water had to be hauled in buckets from a spring at the edge of the forest. This meant trudging through the snow for about a quarter of a mile with heavy water buckets, another job for Margo.

The toilet was also an outdoor affair. It was best visited when it did not snow or rain. But even so, it often sported a waiting line, because besides the regular inhabitants of the house, there now was also a refugee family from the French border who had been taken in.

So it was indeed fortunate that Margo broke her ankle in December instead of during the summer. The wood was home, most of it was sawed, split, and set up. But despite all the misery the mood was happy.

Margo's suitcase had disgorged riches beyond imagination. There was even a piece of cloth, which was turned into a dress for Sigrid. And there was flour, lard, rice, noodles, plus two more priceless items, a pound of sugar, and a chunk of chocolate. There was enough to even bake a cake. This then was a rich Christmas indeed at the Schneider household.

# 26

Back in America I had a soft life. The team of sixteen scientists was complete and we were driven to Stapleton Airport in Colorado Springs to be flown to Annapolis, Maryland. There was a lot of grumbling at the airport by the civilians as they watched the German POWs boarding a military plane. In order for them to get a plane ticket, they had to stand in line for hours, and maybe even till the next day.

We flew in an old clunker of a US Air Force transport and finally landed in Chattanooga, Tennessee, for refueling. By this time the guard and we were on buddy-buddy terms, sharing endless stories and cigarettes, even being treated to candy bars and a bottle of coke. So it was no great surprise to us when the guard told us in Chattanooga to run along, but to make sure to be back in time for take-off, about three hours later. What a guy. No way could we take him up on his generous but foolish offer and possibly get him into trouble. Instead, we snoozed a bit while the plane was being serviced.

When we arrived early the next morning we were given nice quarters where we even had a hot shower. We snacked a bit from the trays of food we found on a table, then fell asleep. At noon, and then again in the evening, we were waited on like in a restaurant by white-clad German POWs who wondered what kind of special guests we were.

After another day of rest we were bussed to Fort George Meade, Maryland. There we were put into the former stockade on the Army base. Every day we were served our meals banquet style, all real Army chow delivered straight from the base kitchen. We were told to stay in the compound and wait for further instructions, which should be forthcoming shortly. We waited day after day, but nothing happened except breakfast, lunch, and dinner. That meant that during the day we were left to our own devices. In the evenings we went exploring since there was never a guard on duty. So it was only natural that we wound up at the canteen, much to the surprise of the GIs there.

We had been issued nice US Army uniforms and the POW letters on the sleeves of our uniforms were fairly small. It always took a while till some GI caught on to the fact that we were indeed German POWs, and that we were loose on the Army Base. Not having any money was no problem. We were not the enemy any more, we were celebrities who were going to assist the US against the Japs and the Reds and we were treated accordingly. They told their stories, we told ours, and a good time was had by all.

Then one day an Army captain appeared shortly after breakfast, accompanied by a balding civilian. The captain told us to assemble at a certain building within ten minutes for training. As we entered we saw sixteen tables and chairs, neatly arranged at one end of the huge room. Each table sported a big, black, ugly, old Underwood typewriter.

Here we not only learned that the quick brown fox jumped over the fence, but also that the quick movement of the enemy jeopardized six of our gunboats. This we learned from the elderly civilian who greeted us cordially, and then explained: 'The Army in its infinite wisdom has decreed that I teach you German fellows touch-typing. The time allotted is two hours, so let's begin at once.'

My time at the Naval Academy was great fun, but all good times will finally come to an end. We were transferred back to the POW camp at Ft. George Meade to be repatriated. We were bored stiff in the camp and volunteered for work, any kind of work.

The first assignment we drew was a trip to the so-called slave market. This place was at a junction of two minor roads, which sported a rundown café with a gas pump out front. A truckload of POWs would be driven there in the morning to be distributed to the local farmers. The farmers typically would stand next to their old pickups and motioned the guard how many POWs they wanted.

I liked the looks of one of the farmers who was asking for three guys by holding up three fingers. So I grabbed two of my buddies and we sauntered over. The farmer motioned us wordlessly into the bed of his pickup and we drove off. Once at his place we were shown to the barn and the pigsty and given shovels before he disappeared, again without a word.

Obviously the poor guy was a deaf-mute. We shoveled and scraped, then hosed down the place with water, and at noon, when the farmer returned everything was shipshape.

This time he pointed to the yard behind the house where we found soap and towels laid out on a bench next to the water faucet. We had just finished washing and toweling ourselves, when his wife stepped through the back door to see how we were getting along.

At that very moment the farmer walked around the corner of the house and husband and wife started arguing about what to feed the Krauts. It turned out that he was not a deaf-mute after all.

That started us laughing and we switched into English, telling them that anything they wanted to serve us would be welcome. The poor farmer almost dropped his teeth, he hadn't expected us to speak English, as we had not expected him to speak at all.

After this little episode we became good friends and returned there for over a week, some days only working half a day. We spent time in the woods in the afternoons, or the farmer drove us around the neighborhood to meet other folks and to see a good part of the real America close up.

One other thing I saw close up one afternoon was a bull. The farmer had asked me to drive some cattle to the end of the pasture, where he wanted to let me watch him dehorning his cattle. Everything went fine until I had almost reached my destination, when this particular bull decided he had enough of being bullied by me. First he just quit walking and nothing I did could entice him to go one step further.

I hollered at him, I tried to sweet talk him into moving, but he just stood there like a statue. Maybe he was thinking what to do about this new fellow who was getting quite irksome. At any rate, he finally turned slowly around and looked at me with his beady eyes, then he lowered his head and slowly started towards me. Being a city boy I was not at all wise in the way of handling bulls.

The first thing I did was gauge the distance to the fence, it was definitely too far away for a retreat. That meant that somehow I had to deal with the situation right where I was. By this time the bull was close enough for me to swing the thin long branch I had in my hand right across his snout. He looked very surprised, then turned and trotted on, leaving me with an even more surprised look and a loudly thumping heart.

# 27

I think it's time to take a breather and maybe have a glass of Irish Cream," I suggested.

With this I stopped and turned to Margo, but she was already halfway out of her chair. She had heard the words Irish Cream and those words will get her going any time. After she had filled our four glasses we just sat and chatted for a while, sipping Irish Cream. But not for long. Eddy was anxious for me to continue, so I started up again.

"Another place where I worked was the Jesuit Woodstock College. Our main job there consisted of cleaning the dining hall after meals, removing the dishes, washing the tables, etc. The waste of food was absolutely unbelievable. The serving dishes that were sent back to the dishwashers were often still half full of food. We were told that we were not allowed to eat any of these leftovers, such as scrambled eggs or chicken.

And since there was no military guard with us, the Jesuits posted one of the brothers as guard and overseer. He was to make sure we didn't steal any of the food they were throwing away. But they were no match for our ingenuity. And we had a lot of fun debating whose dictates were to have priority, the orders of the US Army, or their religious tenets.

But the best happened when we one day happened to see two Jesuit brothers sneaking along the basement corridor. They stopped at one the many enclosures that had been built in the basement as storage rooms. My buddy and I could hardly believe our eyes, when we watched them.

Some time before they had obviously loosened a board of the enclosure. As we watched they moved that board to the side, pulled out a piece of tubing and started to suck on it.

We found out the next day that this was the enclosure where the mess wine was kept. From then on we all had a glass or two of wine every evening before leaving for the POW camp.

Later I was sent to the Woodstock College's chicken farm where I did little chores, such as collecting eggs. I also helped once with slaughtering chickens. I don't know how many men the college housed, but I found out that every week they killed 300 chickens for the kitchen. My job that day was to run the defeathering operation.

One man had to grab the chicken, cut off its head, then throw the chicken into a 55-gallon drum. There the headless carcass would be flopping around for a while. Another guy would then immerse the chicken in hot water for a short time before handing it to me. I operated a revolving drum, which had short pieces of rubber garden hose mounted on it at right angles.

These rubber hose pieces made short shrift of the feathers as I held the chicken against them. Fortunately I had this job only once. It was not something I was looking forward to doing again. Not only was I also full of wet feathers at the end, but it also was a very smelly job.

I liked much better working along the road mending fences. This was a fun job. There was no supervision and no guard. I could have taken off into the countryside had I wanted to. Here I could watch the cars go by, the job was not demanding, and it was not a dirty or smelly place. I even had kids come by to talk to me and keep me company.

But the crown of my stint at the college belongs to one afternoon when the guard drove up in his jeep to where I had just finished my job on the fence. 'Come on,' he hollered, 'we are going for a ride.'

Off we went through the woods behind the college and then into a large meadow with low bushes here and there. There he stopped and he told me to watch for rabbits while he chambered some bullets into his carbine. If anybody had been watching they would then have seen a German POW with a US Army carbine shooting rabbits, encouraged by the prisoner's unarmed guard standing at his side."

Eddy posed a question at that point. "Did you ever consider taking off into the countryside and become a civilian and melt into the general population? It would have been easy to do so according to your story."

"No," I answered. "First of all I don't think that I could have disappeared easily into the general population. After all, what did I know about where to go and live, how to act as an American, how to get a job, etc. Some guys thought about it, but all these speculations were just dreams. As for me, the most important reality was that I wanted to get home, not stay in America. And I figured I soon would go home.

# 28

After our one year stint at the Naval Academy had come to an end, and before we were transferred back to the POW camp at Fort George Meade, there was a little farewell party for us. At the end of the party we all were given a letter of appreciation from the State Dept. It stated that we should be repatriated at the earliest date and should receive any necessary assistance to that end. This letter later turned out to be a lifesaver for us indeed.

But let me first tell you about my trip back across the ocean. There were about 2000 German POWs, plus a few hundred French troops. standing on the pier prior to embarkation. And this time we did not sail in a Liberty Ship.

The skipper said a few words and then asked for someone who spoke English. And since never to volunteer is one of the fundamental tenets of Army life, none of us sixteen uttered a word.

Down we went into the hold of the transport, and while I was getting my bunk in order, a US sailor came along and somehow we had words. Now I must add that I spoke English OK, but I also had had a lot of contact with plain GIs and was quite fluent in 'Armyese'. Armyese' is a special language reserved for bad or stressful situations and consists mostly of four-letter words.

Maybe I bumped into that sailor, or he didn't like my nose, at any rate, we went at it full force, verbally that is in Armyese, until he suddenly came to attention. I turned and before me stood the skipper, all 6 feet 6 inches of him, arms akimbo. He almost blew me over when he bellowed at me, 'I asked for a chap who speaks English and I wind up with a ninny. And then there is this guy here who speaks English fluently. Get your ass up on the bridge on the double, both of you.' And with this he turned and stalked off.

I don't know what happened to the sailor after he delivered me, but I was told to stay, but stay out of the way. I was told that this would be my place during the day, so that they had somebody available if they needed an interpreter. But they liked my English with the German accent, and so I was given more to do.

That was how come I spent the entire trip to France on the bridge, calling out the POWs at chow time, doing the Navy singsong every morning about 'man the broom handle - sweep clean fore and aft', and so on. Naturally, I couldn't go to lunch or dinner with the rest of the POWs, so I had to contend myself with going to the officer's mess later and bother the chef there to cook me a medium steak.

This was the one and only time I remember when volunteering would have been called for. But after so many years in the military the unspoken rule not to volunteer had become part of me.

It was an otherwise uneventful crossing in stark contrast to the crossing a year before. Once we arrived in LeHavre we were put on trucks to be driven in a convoy to a huge POW camp somewhere on the outskirts of town.

It was a slow process to load a large number of trucks, so we POWs had nothing to do but enjoy the scenery in the harbor from the vantage point up in the Army trucks, just talking and smoking our Camels. We also wondered why a fair number of Frenchmen kept walking around among our trucks.

When the realization finally hit us we knew what to do. Instead of smoking our cigarettes all the way to the end, we smoked them only halfway before throwing the large cigarette butts overboard. The Frenchmen eagerly bent down to pick them up, and then they would bow to us with a 'merci bien, monsieur'.

This then was our revenge of sorts. Because a year before, when we left France, we had been driven like cattle through the city of Marseille with the French lining the streets as if this was a parade. They threw flowers at us from the sidewalks and also from the apartment windows above. We probably would have enjoyed the flowers had the pots been removed first.

# 29

# THE POSTWAR YEARS

The POW camp, where we wound up, was huge. It consisted of a number of smaller fenced in units with alleys for guards and vehicle traffic between them. We were assigned a comfortable Army tent equipped with Army bunk beds, and even the food was good. We were in good spirits, because we knew that we soon would be home with our families.

After four or five days of waiting we were finally called out and were marched to another camp unit. There were about four hundred POWs lined up. We were added to their column and were then marched to still another large camp unit.

There we expected to be processed for repatriation because here was a large tent. We saw what appeared to be medical personnel who had the POWs ahead of us remove their shirts before examining them. Our turn came soon and we also had to remove our shirts and proceed past some white clad Frenchmen who looked us over and pronounced us fit.

This baffled us, and so we asked one of the POWs who worked there as orderly what this was all about. He told us that the entire contingent was to be sent to work in some French copper mines someplace.

The group elected me as their spokesperson and I confidently approached a US Army Tech Sgt. who seemed to be in charge. I told him that we were told in the US that we would be sent home without delay, and then showed him my letter from the State Department.

He looked it over and frowned. Did anyone else have this kind of letter he wanted to know. I told him, sure, we all did. He wanted to see all of them and collected them. Next he tore up the letters we had handed over to him and threw the pieces away. Then he turned back to us and laughed and told us that we would go where he would send us. And it would be a long time from now till we would go home. At any rate, the State Department was a long ways away in another country on the other side of the Atlantic.

After that the whole unfortunate lot, including us, was marched off to the compound from where the main contingent had come. It was on the way back that we noticed a jeep with a US officer slowly driving along the alley between the compounds.

We started hollering in English for him to stop so we could talk to him. He stopped at once to find out what this bunch of English speaking POWs was all about. We told him in detail about our letters from the State Department and what had happened in the examination tent.

An MP was sent to the big tent to try to retrieve enough of the evidence. He soon came back with a few shreds of paper, which the colonel examined closely. Then the colonel assured us that we would soon be on our way home.

A few minutes later a sheepish Tech Sgt. appeared and apologized profusely. The Colonel ordered him to move us sixteen to a special compound and put us on the next POW train to Germany. We were overjoyed and gratefully thanked the Colonel.

The Sgt. wordlessly marched us to an empty compound where we slept soundly until about five the next morning. It was our nemesis again, the Tech Sgt., who roused us. 'Now you will be going where I tell you. And it is not home, you bastards,' he snarled before marching us off, just as it was getting light.

But fate intervened again, and as on the day before, a jeep came driving along. Once more we screamed and hollered in English, and by a million in one chance, here was the same Colonel.

Several MPs arrived shortly, the Tech Sgt. was led off to somewhere, and we were turned over to two MPs with the explicit order to get us on the very next train to Germany. And I think it was less than five hours later that we were rolling towards home."

At that point my friend Bill had a question. "After a close call like that one must have been - I don't know, happy is not the right word – it must have felt like miracles still do happen from time to time. Any idea what happened to those other guys that were going to the French copper mines?"

"Not really, Bill," I answered him. "We heard some rumors. One said that the US stepped in and told the French that the US would not allow that, that those were POWs that had been captured by American Forces. Another rumor said that they came home after about another six months. I really don't know. Either rumor could have been true.

We were only too glad that we were not among them and were going home. And as we were rolling through France our train picked up several POWs that appeared from somewhere. Probably escaped from a POW camp in France. And would you believe it, none of the US guards moved a finger.

Anyway, there were quite a few more German POWs on the train when we arrived in Germany than there had been when we boarded the train in France.

As to me, I had butterflies in my stomach. I was on my way home and soon I would be with Margo. It was a sunny day, even the weather cooperated, and I mean it was sunny in more than one way.

# 30

And so I returned from the USA in June of 1946, on a warm, summer day. I was now a civilian again. I had made my way to Weinheim, at the edge of the Odenwald, in order to take the little steam engine train up to the town close to Schimmeldewog. I did not know that the tunnel under the Kreidach Pass had been dynamited by retreating German troops.

One of the roads leading into the Odenwald crossed over the train tracks right next to the little train station. And as I was waiting at the train station I could hear a train's bell and its whistle in the distance. It was arriving from up in the mountains I assumed.

The bells at the crossing started clanging away, and the barrier slowly came down to close the crossing to traffic just when a US Army truck drove up and stopped at the crossing gate.

When I saw that truck I at once hightailed over to see if I could hitch a ride with them instead of taking the train. There were two GIs in the cab and they seemed to be happy to have somebody on board who knew the territory in case they got lost. That's how I arrived in Schimmeldewog in style in my own private taxi, because that was exactly where they were headed.

The truck's destination was the sawmill at the foot of the hillside where my father's house stood. From here a small path ran towards the creek. There was a small bridge you crossed to get to a steep and rocky little path, which ran up the side of the mountain to Dad's house.

The emotions at that moment when I arrived there are impossible to describe, - joy, relief, apprehension, doubts, all mixed together in one incredible jumble.

What changes had happened here? What about Margo and our child. Was it a boy or a girl. Had they made it through the war safely? What about my father and his wife Marie? What about the house, was it still standing?

Margo naturally did not know that I had returned from the USA. She had had only one communication from me, the official notification that I was alive, that I had been captured, and that I was not injured. That one card from the Red Cross had come after a long period of silence when no one knew what had happened to my outfit. She knew only that my unit had ceased to exist, and no one knew if there were any survivors. But Margo steadfastly refused to give up hope, not only that, there was not the slightest doubt in her mind that I was alive."

I stopped here when I saw Helen turn to Margo. "Whoa, you must be a strong women to endure all this and not break down. I admire you."

"There is nothing superwomenish about that," Margo replied, "you just have to take each day as it comes. And at any rate, there were all these other folks who depended on me. You will be surprised what you can do when you absolutely have to."

Well, besides being in love, I also admired Margo for more reasons than I can list here. But it was time to get on with our story.

"It was during that time of not knowing what had happened to me that Margo had gone to the village one day on an errand. And while she was talking with one of the local storekeepers, the question popped up as to what happened to her husband Wolfgang.

When Margo corrected the storekeeper and told her that her husband's name was Horst, it started a lively debate. Everyone pitched in to agree with the storekeeper. Yes, they all knew Wolfgang as a boy, when he visited his father once in a while.

I had never mentioned the name Wolfgang to Margo since I had not known of anyone by that name in my family. Therefore the whole thing was a huge mystery to Margo. Surely, if I had had a brother, I would have told her about him.

There obviously was some kind of misunderstanding. In fact, it was funny in a way, because it was the first of April, and Margo could hardly wait to return home to tell this April Fool's joke to Marie, my father's wife.

Marie's reaction was far from laughter. She was quiet for a while and then told Margo, yes, Horst indeed has a half brother by the name of Wolfgang. A child borne of a union after Horst's father and mother had divorced. But Horst's father and Wolfgang's mother never did marry, and in fact, she was not living anymore. This then is how Wolfgang later came to be known as the 'April Fool's Joke' among the three of us, Marie, Margo, and myself.

Wolfgang turned up at the house not long after Marie's explanation. He came straight to Schimmeldewog after he was released from a POW camp in Italy. He did not endear himself to Marie or Margo, or to me, when I met him later. He always seemed to feel superior to everyone, and he let us know how he felt. It was no wonder then that very few words passed between Margo and Wolfgang.

But on a certain warm, summer day in June of 1946, he had to talk to her. My father sent him to deliver a message to Margo to return from the village where she had gone to see the dentist. Naturally, Margo wanted to know what was so urgent that she had to give up her dentist's appointment, but he did not know, he claimed.

Margo packed up her ever-present knitting and hurried home. Hurried probably is not the correct term, because she was still walking slowly with the help of a cane because of her broken and incorrectly set right ankle.

As she approached the sawmill she had to pass by a lady who eked out a meager living by selling some grocery staples out of her living room. Just then Margo saw Wolfgang making a hand movement to that lady as if he wanted her to not talk to Margo. Now Margo was doubly curious as to why there was such urgency.

A good thing, too, she thought, that the US Army truck was gone from in front of the sawmill. Earlier, as she had crossed the creek next to the sawmill, on the way to the dentist, she almost had come face to face with this US Army truck. She had ducked into the nearest house entrance to hide and avoid the enemy vehicle.

After she crossed the creek she could see Marie and my father standing on the small porch, which overlooked the valley. Both were looking down at her, Marie holding Sigrid, everyone smiling.

There must have been some good news, Margo thought, maybe from Horst. And with that thought in her mind she pushed her heavy knitting bag at Wolfgang, threw away her cane, and crawled, slid, and clawed her way up the rocky path to the house.

Many times before this day I had pictured in my mind my homecoming, me rushing up to the house where a smiling Margo opened her arms to me, embracing me after two years of absence. But this was not what really happened, Margo was not standing with open arms on the balcony, instead there was a young lady encrusted with dirt, crawling up to the house on all fours."

Giggles from the two women interrupted my story. And then Bill said: "I only hope you had a chance to take pictures. What a memento that would be."

Shaking his head he then turned to his wife. "You know Hon, these two don't do anything simple and normal. Remember, when I came home from Korea I phoned you, I came home, we hugged and laughed and cried a bit. Then I took a shower, I dressed, and later we went out to dinner."

"That's just it," chimed in Eddy's wife. "That's why their stories are so fascinating." I just smiled and went on with my story telling.

# 31

"Now that I was finally home I first stayed in Schimmeldewog for some time since there was no job to be had in my field. And getting my education was utterly out of the question, the daily bread came first.

I finally got a job in Mannheim as an interpreter with a US Army unit during the daytime, and on weekend nights I freelanced as a photographer on the Army base.

This was the time when segregation was still the order of the day and the unit where I worked was still a segregated black battalion. They had an excellent and well-known dance band. They played swing and jitterbug and all kinds of other danceable tunes every Friday, Saturday, and Sunday in the big Army Rec. Hall.

While I worked there as an interpreter I befriended a soldier by the name of Mills, who was a mortician in private life, and he and I formed a partnership. He was in charge of supplying me with the necessary trade items, that is to say cigarettes, soap, nylons, chocolate, etc.,

These I needed to trade for film developing and having prints made. The film itself was bought by my friend Mills in the Army PX. On weekend nights I worked on the dance floor where I would entice the black GIs to have their pictures taken while they were dancing with their white dates.

I charged two dollars for each photo, and after expenses for films and prints, Mills and I split the profit half and half. This then became my main income, and while the dollar amount was relatively small, the pay was in dollars instead of the almost worthless German Mark. We could finally afford some long missed luxuries, such as soap.

Housing was practically non-existent in the heavily bombed city of Mannheim, but I did manage to obtain a single room, paid for with cigarettes, naturally. Since I worked during the week on my regular job as an interpreter, and moonlighted weekends, Margo and I did not have very many chances to see each other. But at least life was a bit more tolerable from a strictly material standpoint.

Then one day, just two weeks before Christmas, I was rudely awakened early in the morning. Two German policemen burst into my room. My room was thoroughly searched and I was arrested and dragged off to the Mannheim prison. It was cold and I was alone in my cell wondering what this was all about, especially since there had not been a search or arrest warrant.

I was unable to talk to anyone. My pleas to the jail wardens to see a lawyer or at least contact my family fell on deaf ears. Well, those were not regular times, and procedures were not always followed. Or maybe the mindset of the police was still of the totalitarian variety.

When I did not come home the next weekend as I had promised Margo, she went to Mannheim to search for me. There my landlady told her the sad story of my arrest almost two weeks ago.

It took Margo only a short time to hunt down Mills, and together they went to the US military Judge Advocate's office. That office, naturally, had no record of me.

Margo was pregnant at the time, and as always, looked much more pregnant than she really was. She also put on a super show, as if she was ready to have a baby right there in the office, so they promised to search for me.

The story of how she sprung me I found out later, after my release, in the early afternoon of Christmas Eve. The metal door to my cell suddenly opened and a warden with a gruff voice told me to follow him. We went down and up some stairs and along several hallways until we finally arrived at the US military liaison office.

There they wanted to know why I was arrested, who did the arresting, what kind of arrest orders I had been shown, etc., etc. Naturally, I had no answer to any of their questions, and they told me that they had been unable, either, to find out why I had been held for two weeks.

The whole affair, I learned later, had been set in motion by a young lady who had had designs on me and who I had offended by not paying attention to her.

Let me see if I can remember the name of that poet who came up with a good saying about such situations. I think it was a fellow by the name of Congrave, or something similar. I probably can not quote him verbatim but I might come close. He said: 'Heaven has no Rage like Love to Hatred turned, nor Hell a Fury, like a Woman scorned'.

Considering the sad state of public transportation at that time, I was lucky to still make it home that night, arriving shortly after midnight. The last miles were on foot and they were cold, long, and dark, but the thought of Margo and everyone else in the house, plus Christmas, made me walk that stretch in record time.

We enjoyed the holidays till after New Year when I had to go back to Mannheim and report to the office of the US Judge Advocate. There I finally found out a few clues as to why I had had to spend fourteen miserable and cold days in prison.

I actually had become acquainted with this prison before, when I had spent three days there due to an error of records, a mistaken identity. But at that time someone apologized to me for the error and I agreed that such errors could easily happen during such turbulent times.

It was easy to get arrested during the years right after the war. All kinds of patrols roamed the city during the day, but especially during the night; US military jeeps, German police, as well as mixed patrols of German police, American MPs, plus one or two Polish refugees. And many times I was hailed by a roving American MP jeep patrol as I was walking home after leaving the dance hall at two in the morning.

It usually went something like this: 'Kommen Sie her, Ihr Passport, bitte.' I in turn answered in English and showed my German papers. This provoked a question like: 'Where did you get this ID, what is your unit.' Sometimes I could convince the patrol that I was indeed a German civilian and not an AWOL GI, but many times I could not.

When I couldn't I was arrested and driven to the headquarters of the MP where the duty officer would give me a tongue lashing for again speaking English. He told me to just talk German the next time so that his guys wouldn't pick me up. Regulations required that the MP now drive me home. Free taxi service so to speak."

"Why were there so many patrols running around, the war was over, wasn't it." It was Helen asking that question.

"Because there was much lawlessness, Helen. Renegade German ex-soldiers roamed the countryside, many of them having lost their entire family during the war. Many others were displaced persons who were at loose ends, having lost their homes behind the Russian lines. Some were Nazis who didn't want to go where they were known, and some were outright criminals, such as the SS guards from the concentration camps

I am sorry, Helen, to explain all this will take too long to explain, we better go on."

# 32

The German police who had searched my room when they arrested me, had found one item that could have gotten me in deep trouble, a full carton of Camel cigarettes. The possession of American cigarettes was illegal according to German law, it was considered a sign of black market activity. As it was, this carton belonged to my friend Mills.

It was Christmas Eve when the German police finally turned me over to the US military justice system. And since the German police still had not filed a formal complaint at that time, the US court later returned this carton of cigarettes to me.

Maybe the Americans felt sorry for me, or for whatever reason, they gave the cigarettes back to me. I also had now a letter on the official letterhead of the Judge Advocate, stating that I was in legal possession of one carton of American cigarettes. Luckily for me, the letter didn't mention the brand of cigarettes.

I was going to wind up in prison one more time; that time out of pure stupidity. And I think I should tell you about that in a little while.

At any rate, neither this prison time, nor the other two times were entered into my records.

But something good came from the last episode, I now had an invaluable letter. As I have just said, at this time it was a crime for a German to possess American cigarettes. But from here on I could walk the streets with a carton of cigarettes in my satchel without fear of the police arresting me for illegal possession of American cigarettes. A carte blanche.

The third time I spent time in this prison was quite hilarious, at least in retrospect. It all started one night after I had left my job at the dance hall. As I rounded the next street corner I ran into a mixed patrol. The German police displayed their proficiency again by trying to arrest me. This time because I was wearing a pair of US Army low quarter shoes.

But a few words with the MPs changed the situation. The MPs made it clear to the German police that they would handle this situation, and then they promptly arrested me. So, instead of having to spend the rest of the night at the German police station, the MPs let me spend that time with them at their station. I think that the camera, and the promise of having their pictures taken did the trick.

I was extremely lucky that night because I still had my night's receipts in my pocket in the form of US Military script money. If this had been found on me I would have faced no less than three years in jail without parole. But I was able to smuggle the money to one of the GIs who I knew and who had stopped at our little group to find out what the problem was.

The night at the MP station was not a bad experience, we played cards, told stories, and drank black coffee till it was time in the morning for them to drive me to the US Court. They even wrangled me a speedy appearance before the judge, after all, by now we were almost buddies. And I always wondered if they even put in a good word for me with the military judge.

Having read a few American murder mysteries came in very handy this day because I immediately asked the judge in English if I could address the bench. When he told me to go ahead I said: 'If it pleases the Court I would like to have the hearing conducted without the assistance of an interpreter since I am quite capable to express myself in English.' This then was granted and we proceeded.

Judge: 'You stand accused of illegal possession of US Army property, to wit, one pair of GI low quarter shoes. Where did you get them?'

I explained: 'Your Honor, I possess only one pair of shoes, which are presently for repairs at the shoemaker's, and in order to go to work I borrowed this pair of shoes from a GI friend of mine.'

J.: 'The prisoner will step up to the bench.'

When I did this, the judge leaned close to me and told me that I wouldn't gain anything by bringing my GI friend into the picture, but would probably cost him a court martial. This said he told me to step back.

J.: 'Now I want the truth out of you. Where did you get these shoes?'

I had to think fast and then answered: 'Your Honor, the truth is, I found them behind a trash can.'

J.: 'Let the record show he found them behind a trash can. And you, young man, step up to the bench.'

For the second time I approached the judge who lowered his voice again as he informed me that he would have to sentence me to three days in jail, the minimum sentence allowed. But, he cautioned, if I pleaded innocent, I would be in jail for another two to three months, while I waited for a trial in the next higher court. There they gave out no less than fourteen days, which did not appeal to me. With this he had me step back again.

J.: 'How do you plead?'

What could I say but 'Guilty, your Honor.'

We all now rose and I received my sentence of three days, reduced to two since he gave me credit for the night spent playing cards with the MPs.

But once more, now for the third time, he called me forward to face him at close range. And then he leaned towards me and whispered conspiratorially, 'You better use some black shoe polish on those shoes, the police look only for brown shoes.'

With this he calmly sat down again, raised his arm and hollered to the warden: 'Take him away.'

Now the story rightfully should end here, but it does not, because when I was let out of the prison, I still wore the same illegal GI low quarter shoes.

And so, I made my way back to the battalion's barracks on foot after my release from the prison, always on the lookout for roving military jeep patrols. I certainly was not anxious for    a repeat performance. I was even afraid to use the streetcar since that would have exposed me unnecessarily to public scrutiny.

It was late afternoon when I finally arrived at the gate where a burly black MP greeted me with a big smile and a question. 'Hey, Slim, where you been, we all missed you.'

When I explained to him what had happened and that I had spent two days in the now familiar prison he roared with laughter. I told him that it was not funny at all. He said, yes, it was, I should have known better, living with the US Army, as it was.

Then he reached in his pocket, pulled out some keys on a key ring and said: 'Get your ass up to my quarters, get into my footlocker and grab the black shoe polish you find there and blacken those *&#@* shoes.'

And while it were the MPs who arrested me for possession of brown shoes, it were again the MPs who gave me their own black shoe polish to change them to black. It was a confused and confusing time, I only hope I didn't confuse you too much."

## 33

I was getting a bit tired talking so long. And also I had to excuse myself to go and get rid of some of the coffee I had had for lunch.

I returned just when Margo was telling them that she had never dreamed to be married to a jailbird. And since it was too late now to change the situation she would keep me out of pity. After the laughter died down I resumed where I had left off.

"Eventually my friend and partner Mills was transferred to Stuttgart. This meant that I also had to move to Stuttgart. And it meant that getting home to see Margo and our daughter for even a short visit now became a major problem, and my trips home became very infrequent.

It was not just the distance, but the fact that you needed a permit to travel, which I could not get since I was not legally in Stuttgart. The only legal travel without a travel permit was local travel. Let me tell you what I had to do to come home to Margo for seven hours.

After I finished work shortly after midnight I would walk to the train station, about 45 minutes away. There I would buy a platform permit. These platform permits were available to allow family members or friends onto the train platform to wave their good-byes.

Once on the platform I had to position myself strategically fairly close to the front end of the platform, waiting for the train to pull out. As it gathered speed I had to wait for the right moment to start running to match the speed of the train. That was easy. The trick was to match the speed just when there was a break between two railcars next to me.

German rail cars, both freight and passenger cars, have at their ends on either side big round bumpers, and a ladder to get to the roof. A quick jump at the right moment had me standing on the bumper, holding on to the ladder. It was a bold and dangerous maneuver, but I was still young and invincible. Or so I thought.

It was not first class travel, having the wind in your hair, as well as the cinders from the steam locomotive. And in winter it was cold and miserable. But there was no other way.

In the morning I would arrive in Mannheim where I took the local electric train to the next city where I changed to the little steam engine train into the mountains. At the end of the line I started hiking through the woods across a small mountain pass. I arrived home about midnight.

Seven hours later, in the morning, I had to start again on my trip back. I would arrive in the evening just in time to go to work. Sometimes the pass I had to cross on my way back had snow and the walking was cold, wet and miserable. But I was in love and my sweetheart was waiting.

Horst Schneider

A few times Margo persuaded me in the morning to stay another day and I remember with pleasure that it did not take a lot of persuasion. In fact, I guess that just a small hint could do the trick.

# 34

But finally Mills was transferred back to the US and I had to find something else to do.

In Germany existed an unusual business, called a 'Lesezirkel', which could loosely be translated as Reader's Circle. This was, and maybe still is, a business, which bought magazines and periodicals similar to Fortune, Times, Saturday Evening Post, National Geographic, etc, put each into a binder, and then delivered the whole set of about eight or nine magazines and periodicals each week to subscribers.

The subscriber then kept the magazines for one week and exchanged them for the next set a week later. You could subscribe to receive a brand new set every week, or a one week old set, and so on.

The subscription price dropped drastically with the age of the magazines. This way even poor people could get a great variety of periodicals at a rock bottom cost. All this was before television, when people were still reading instead of gawking.

There was a national company, which operated in Mannheim, and we decided that we would get into this business as a local competitor.

Horst Schneider

Monday mornings I would leave for Mannheim and start my rounds with a special bike. It had a small front wheel with a heavy steel basket mounted above it in which I carried about 70 pounds of magazines. As I delivered my magazines, I would try also to solicit new business. It was hard work riding this clumsy, heavy bike all over town in sunshine, rain, or snow, and then climbing two or three or four stairs to deliver my magazines.

During the week I had to stay someplace in town, but there were no apartments available in town, or even rooms to rent at a price I could afford. Such rooms were strictly black market quarters since all living space was strictly rationed at a fixed square footage per person. If you had a large apartment that exceeded one's entitlement you had to give up apartment space to people who had lost their living quarters.

But I finally found a place I could rent cheaply. It was an old chicken coop. I had to clean it out first, but it had a roof and a door and a window.

It was about eight feet long and maybe four feet wide, with a window in one of the long sides. Along the opposite wall I built a bench, which was my bed and my chair. Under the window I mounted a wide board, which became my table. Here I could do my paperwork, assemble the binders, etc.

For warmth I wore sweaters, a candle served as my chandelier, and old newspapers kept me warm at night. It would have been nice to have had a mattress and a blanket, but those luxuries were not available then. Even at home in Schimmeldewog we slept on a straw mattress.

I was in my mid twenties then and just surviving was plenty enough to be happy about. I had survived the war, I was in one piece, in good health, and I had the best wife to stand by my side. Life was good to me.

Mannheim had been bombed heavily and many streets were still closed to traffic. Men and women had turned out voluntarily to clear the streets of bricks and other debris, which was then loaded into mine lorries. Those were then pushed along on hastily laid tracks to the outskirts of town where mountains of debris accumulated. All this was later recycled into new bricks and other building material.

But there was one sprawling residence, which had suffered only minor bomb damage. It was located in the western part of the town and had been the residence of the once ruling aristocracy.

One day Margo came to visit me and I took her along on an errand to that place. There were a number of huge rooms on ground level. Some where obviously reception rooms, what the others were for I couldn't figure out. None were lived in since that area had been declared some kind of museum or heritage area.

She was waiting for me to return, sitting in one of the huge, now empty reception rooms at ground level, and looking out through the low, wide, high, open patrician windows.

Through one of these windows, right across the windowsill, stepped a huge male Great Dane, and approached her, eyeing the sandwich she was eating. She told me later that this dog was absolutely the largest she had ever seen, and I had to believe her. Would she otherwise have volunteered to share her meager lunch with him?"

Margo stood up and showed us how high the windowsill was.

"Yes," she told us, "it was a huge, huge beast, almost like a small horse. Now, I love animals and they love me generally, and that's a good thing or else I would have freaked out.

As it was, the dog didn't look menacing and he even let me have my half of our lunch."

I thought I saw Helen shiver just a little at the thought of meeting such a creature, but I could have been wrong.

But Margo's remarks gave me an idea.

"Speaking of food," I started up again, "I think that maybe this would be a good time to tell you a little of the food situation in Germany during the first few years of the postwar era."

# 35

"Have you ever been hungry? I mean hungry for a whole week, or a whole month, so hungry you ate weeds? If not, then you did not live in Germany between 1944 and 1947.

In 1945, '46, and '47, the ration for meat, or any kind of meat products, was 100 grams, that is 4 oz., per person per week. You had a choice of meat, or bacon, or fish, or sausage, in other words, any kind of meat product. Nowadays we eat a quarter pound hamburger for lunch, and even order French Fries with it. Imagine, a whole week's ration shot eating just one burger.

Sugar, flour, butter, margarine, and all other staples were strictly rationed also. Potatoes and other vegetables were very scarce. Margo was lucky to live in the country. She had a chance to help her neighbors carrying home the hay in summer and doing other chores for them. Many of the men did not come home from the war. Of those that returned, many were wounded. So the small farmers could use all the help they could get.

Carrying hay was done by first piling it on a large tarp, knotting the four corners, and then placing the full tarp on your head. You had to be surefooted with your heavy load, the paths down off the mountain meadows were steep. Not something people would consider doing nowadays, even for apples or peaches or whatever.

The few extra potatoes she had she either got by bartering or she had dug them up from some field at midnight. Potatoes were very important for two reasons. Margo never bought bread, because the way the rations were set up, it was much more economical to bake your own bread. And a potato or two could stretch the meager flour ration even further.

Then there was another reason. Margo sometimes had only water, salt, and a few carrots available. She would add to the water a grated potato to thicken it so it looked almost like soup. And pronto, she had prepared another lunch or dinner.

How to augment the meager rations was always on your mind. I still vividly remember our walks through the woods after I came back from the US, looking for mushrooms and edible wild plants. One particular mushroom we liked grew in a moist place. We never found out its name but when Margo prepared this mushroom it tasted almost like beef.

We also found Chanterelles and many different kinds of Boletes, such as Steinpilz, one of our favorites. We not only added to our meager diet, but at the same time we got an education in identifying mushrooms and plants. This came in handy later when we went mushroom hunting in Colorado.

We found that a number of weeds could be prepared like spinach and tasted very good, which was no surprise since everything tastes good if you are really hungry. Among the weeds we ate, the lowly sting nettle you find next to roads was our favorite by far. I would love to have some cooked even today if we could find them here in Arizona.

Margo had many kitchen tricks she learned by trial and error or by listening to the old folks. For instance, she made something that tasted almost like lard. A slice of bread with this concoction spread on and some salt on top was heavenly.

Of tremendous help also was the garden that Marie, my father's second wife, planted every spring. There grew cabbage, which was sliced, then salted, and finally kept in a large earthenware crock as sauerkraut. Then there were also string beans, which could be salted in a similar fashion.

Wild berries were another gift of the woods. I already told you how Margo used them for trading. In the fall another food source became available. On both sides of the road from the nearest town, where the train station was located, grew apple and pear trees. You could buy from the government the right to the harvest of some of these trees. The price was not steep and many people of the village used this program.

The vast majority of people during that time were slim and trim, obesity was unknown. Today many people pay great sums of money for slimming diets. That is stupid, because we know of a diet program that has been tested for several years and is guaranteed to work. Best of all, we will give it away for free."

# 36

Sally started to laugh and playfully patted Bill's tummy. "Thanks for that diet hint," she giggled. "In the future I will stock my refrigerator with the ingredients and the quantities Horst suggested, and we should have Bill's weight down to a manageable level in no time, right Bill? When do you want me to start?" Bill found it best to ignore her stab and I continued.

"Now that we have established Bill's new diet, let's move on to another subject to round out the picture of the postwar period that you wanted to know about.

In Mannheim there used to be a four-story house that was typical for all the apartment buildings in the larger German cities. They all had the same basic shape of a square U when viewed from above. The open part of the U was connected by a wall, forming a courtyard, and the closed end faced the street.

The building I am talking about had been bombed and the left half of the house, when viewed from the front, was completely gone. The upper two stories of the right wing had burned, but part of the second floor had only slight fire damage and could be fixed up with some work. The main stairs were still intact, but the landings were gone.

The owner was agreeable to my plan to try and make the second floor livable, and so we started on the roof. Some old 55-gallon steel barrels were cut open lengthwise, then flattened and nailed onto the roof. At least the rain and snow could do no further damage.

There was just one room left of the second floor apartment, plus the kitchen, a long hallway, and at the end of the hallway, a toilet, that is, just a stool. Below the toilet was the work area of the old owner of the apartment building where he rebuilt bicycles. Since there were wide cracks in the flooring you could drop paper balls through the cracks and if you had a good aim, the missile might find its target. The old man fortunately had a good sense of humor.

One wall of the kitchen had split, with one half leaning north while the other half was leaning south. A car jack and some four by fours finally put that wall together again. Then came the laborious task of plastering the ceiling and the walls with some old-fashioned gypsum, the kind you mix with water in a bucket and then apply to the wall. You then have just 30 seconds to work it, period. I sweated a lot in this kitchen.

The one room, which was somewhat intact, faced the street and was to be the kids' room. We furnished it with a small potbelly stove, one single small bed for our son Dieter, and one bunk bed for daughters Sigrid and Doris. The window glass was still in its frame, but something had put a hole in it and the glass pieces were leaning this way and that. A bolt and nut through the center with washers on either side provided an easy repair.

149

The door to the room had lost its panels and only the frame was left, quite wobbly without the center panels. This also was easy to repair. We glued brown wrapping paper on both sides, and then sprayed the paper with water to shrink it. After that the door was almost as good as new as long as the kids did not walk through the paper or put their arms through it. I think we had to repair the door only once.

The front door had burned away, but there was enough scrap lumber in the building to build a frame of sorts, into which we fitted the toilet door. Since the toilet was at the very end of the long hallway, around the corner behind the kitchen, its door wasn't missed.

Just a bit more work on the electrical system, and a bit more work on the plumbing made the apartment marginally livable again.

The kitchen saw triple duty, as kitchen, as living room, and as our bedroom. In the corner to the left of the door as you entered were a small footlocker and our bed. This was a wooden frame with a straw mattress, which had to be fluffed up every morning. Against the end of the bed stood an old cupboard with its back to the bed. This held all of Margo's utensils, pots and pans, the china, and the food staples. There was no refrigeration, so we bought milk daily and then stored it in the cool basement.

To the right of and behind the door, as you entered the kitchen, was our table. And since there was not enough room for chairs, we had stools, which could be shoved under the table. Next along the right wall in the far right corner was a combination coal/wood stove. The wall facing the door sported a kitchen table, and the left far corner held the sink.

The sink was about 15 by 24 inches of granite, hollowed out about two inches deep. The water faucet was fairly high above the center of the sink at the end of the cold water pipe jutting out from the wall. The single window was right behind the sink.

Every Saturday we heated a batch of water and the kids got their bath in production line fashion. After the first had been soaped and washed, she was dunked under the cold-water faucet in the sink to be rinsed off. She was then passed to Dad who toweled and rubbed her dry and hopefully warm again, while Mom was already tending to the next.

It was close living, especially during the cold seasons, when the snow blew in around the front door. But we were together, we had our own apartment instead of having to live with two other generations. And we were young and resilient. So we appreciated what we had and we were happy.

And every once in a while I look back and I see that kitchen-bedroom-livingroom combination in my minds eye and it then occurs to me that we were at least as happy there and then as we are now in a nice house.

At those times I am also reminded of what a third grader in Colorado Springs once told her teacher. The teacher had asked her third graders what the difference was between a house and a home. One girl came up with a wonderful explanation: 'The house is outside, the home is inside.' How true.

The only time I had some misgivings about our new quarters was at the time of Margo's first visit to her future castle in the city. Climbing the main stairs you came abruptly to where the second floor landing used to be and you suddenly stood at the edge of the house, looking out into empty space. With the landing in place you could have turned left past the stairs leading to the next floor and there would have been the apartment entrance.

Later on we had a platform of boards in lieu of the landing, but when Margo arrived there was only the beginning of a support structure plus two boards. One board led at an angle away from the last stair step to a support beam eight feet away, the second board spanned the distance from the support beam back to the house and the apartment entrance.

Margo took one long look and then bravely but gingerly tightrope walked across the first board, turned at the end, and balanced across the second board into the apartment. There she stood for a long moment, slowly letting out the breath she had been holding.

The space next to the building, where formerly another apartment building had stood, as well as the missing half of ours, had been cleared and was now a children's playground.

This was greatly appreciated by all parents of the neighborhood since it helped to keep the kids away from the buildings across the street from us, which at the time still contained some unexploded bombs. No wonder then that we expected explicit obedience from our kids when we told them to stay away from those ruins."

Here Sally interrupted me. "How long did you live under those conditions in that burned out building. And if you have any photos of it I would love to see it."

"Let me see, Sally," I answered her. "I think we lived there about four or five years." I turned to

Margo to see what she thought. "Is that about right, sweetheart?" I wanted to know.

She thought for a moment and then nodded agreement.

And turning back to Sally I told her, yes, we have one photo. By this time Margo had already left to find it. She passed it around so everyone could inspect it, and pointed out our apartment and the window of our kids' room.

I waited till the head shaking stopped before going on.

"We went back to this place in 1996, but nothing remained. The entire district had been razed and then rebuilt according to a new plan, not even the streets remained. Even the old horse butcher's place was not there anymore.

# 37

Margo knew him well, she shopped there often, because she received double rations, buying horsemeat. With only four ounces of meat, or any kind of meat product like sausage or bacon, per week per person, this made a huge difference.

My father had told us the story of when he had to eat horsemeat in World War One, and he claimed that he could smell horsemeat from a mile away. Now, it is true without doubt that horsemeat has a slightly different taste from beef, but Margo had become an expert at camouflage, doing quite a bit of magic with her huge collection of herbs and spices.

One day my father and his wife Marie came to Mannheim and had dinner with us. It was a very special occasion and Margo had scrimped here and there to prepare a special dinner in their honor, a dinner crowned by a real pot roast, so Margo said.

A real pot roast was something that had not been seen in Germany for many years. She even had an untrue but believable story concocted as to how she acquired such delicacy. And father swallowed the meat, and the story, and proclaimed it the best pot roast ever to slide across his tongue.

I just remembered a story I have to tell you.

Sometime during the early nineteen fifties the Harlem Globetrotters came to Mannheim for an exhibition game at the downtown stadium. So this then is my story about how Margo broke a long-standing Globetrotter taboo.

At the time I worked in US Intelligence, an outfit that was code named US Air Force Historical Research Division. I had access to a Sears Roebuck catalogue and through my American co-workers I could buy American clothes, which I wore on certain occasions, such as at parties.

My friend and co-worker Eric Friess did likewise and on those occasions we could hardly be told from US citizens. Especially since both of us were addicted to the crossword puzzles in the US paper, the 'Stars and Stripes', which we always carried with us. In fact, since so much during the day happened in English, and all our reports had to be written in English, we spoke English between ourselves most of the time.

The day the Globetrotters came to Mannheim, Margo and I attended an American baseball game on the outskirts of town. We had a good time, even buying hotdogs with military script just like the GIs. And while I was standing in line for my second hot dog, I saw two busses drive in, marked Harlem Globetrotters. I couldn't let this opportunity go by to talk to them, and Margo and I went to investigate.

It turned out that the showers at the downtown stadium were shut off for repairs, which was why they drove out to our baseball arena. It was only natural then that they asked us why we were not going to watch them play downtown. We told them that we did not have tickets. That was no excuse they answered, you can ride to the stadium with us. When Saperstein, the manager, heard that, he almost exploded.

'You guys know the rules, no female rides on our busses, not now, not ever, period,' he hollered, and stalked off. Needless to say, this was a real challenge to the players, and so they did smuggle Margo on board, where she had the time of her life. She sat behind Art Tatum and watched him balance a spinning basketball on his index finger. And later, in the stadium, the team delighted to put on their antics in front of the first row seats where she sat, much to her delight.

But the problem still remained as to how to get into the stadium without tickets. We knew that at the stadium we would have to get past the US guards and the German police. The solution came to me when I saw one of the players getting a cigarette out of a pack of Pall Mall cigarettes. I explained to him what I had in mind and he immediately gave me his cigarettes.

I tore off a square piece of the red outside pack and tucked it in behind my hatband, so that is was just peeking out as if it were a press pass.

We all walked in together, Margo, the players, and I with my Leica camera prominently around my neck. First we just breezed past the German police guards with a curtly 'American Press', and then we nonchalantly waved at the MPs as we passed by with a smile and 'Deutsche Presse'.

The players even wrangled some loge seats for us where we sat enjoying their antics and munching a Wiener on a bun."

# 38

The talk about food gave Margo an idea. She slid out of her armchair, went to the kitchen, and returned with four small plates with assorted cookies. She also refilled our coffee cups.

There was no way for me to continue. The cookies in my lap and the full coffee cup had priority. So we just chatted away about other things for a while before I decided that I was properly fortified and could go on.

"There was an American author whose stories I much enjoyed. His name was Damon Runyan. His stories were set in the roaring nineteen twenties, the prohibition times. One of his colorful characters was named Harry the Horse.

There was also a German character we had nicknamed Harry the Horse. His facial features definitely had something to do with his nickname.

The German Harry the Horse who I will tell you about had risen within the ranks of the postwar Communist Party in Germany to the post of Chief of Propaganda of the German State of Württemberg-Baden.

One afternoon Eric Friess and I looked out the window on the second floor of our HQ building. We were more than surprised when we saw Harry the Horse approach the entrance to our building. Eric raced to the phone immediately to alarm the guard at the entrance. But Harry the Horse just flashed the guard some form of ID and was ushered into the chief's office at once.

What we didn't know at that moment was that Harry the Horse actually had been a mole of ours. He had infiltrated the Communist Party some time ago. And just a few days before he showed up at our offices he had had a rather harrowing experience

The party had found out that he was a mole and had asked him to travel to the Communist East Germany to deliver some supposedly sensitive documents. Naturally, Harry the Horse did not know that his life was at stake.

He was lucky, though. We had found out just in time through another of our moles why he was being sent across the border. We immediately dispatched jeep patrols and a helicopter to intercept him. It was the chopper that located him on the highway only a few miles before the border.

When Harry the Horse spotted the chopper trying to set down ahead of him he panicked and took off for the woods. He was finally located the next morning and returned to the US hospital in Heidelberg, where he had to stay for a day. He was given a different apartment, a new name, and a new identity.

He had now come to our place to inquire about any new assignment. The chief turned him down, because he knew that Harry the Horse had some time ago made arrangements to immigrate to Argentina, and now our office helped him get his immigration expedited.

We had run into Harry the Horse before without realizing it. One day the Communist Party bigwigs were having a celebration and the liquor flowed freely. Harry the Horse slipped them all a Mickey, took the keys from the chief and placed them on the windowsill for us to at once make duplicates. The keys went back to the windowsill and no one of the team ever saw the face of who had supplied the keys for us.

Then it was a hasty trip up to the fifth floor, and from there to the roof. Next came a hair-raising walk along the chimneysweep catwalks to the roof three buildings further, and then off the roof through a small access window in the roof. From there it was a short trip down to the fourth floor. It was an interesting exercise in the dark, especially for someone with acrophobia.

Black curtains were put up to shield the windows, the safe was opened and all pertinent documents were photographed. Including a most interesting list of secret financial contributors.

It was almost seven o'clock in the morning when the work was finally finished and everyone could leave, just as the first employees entered the first floor. It was a close call, but it was well worth the effort."

Here Helen spoke up. "I am very surprised and somewhat perturbed. Some of your stories were not quite legal but they were funny. But this is a different matter. And don't be mad at me if I say how I feel about something like that. Breaking into an office, opening a safe, copying the contents is a criminal activity. Just like Watergate. This I can't condone." She looked very unhappy and somewhat agitated.

This called for an immediate reply.

"Do you think," I addressed her directly, "that blackmailing businesses and individuals into giving money by threat and intimidation is permissible?

Or how about taking over countries by force and other illegal means, as was done in East Germany, the Baltic States, the Czech Republic, Hungary, and so on.

Or depriving millions of people of their freedom in those countries. Those were the issues, life or death of a nation was at stake here.

And I was proud I could play a small part in helping to prevent any further enslavement. Later, not just because of that little story I just told you, the Communist East Germans thought I was worth $50.000. Made me even prouder. But it added to the other reasons we had to leave the country. I was endangering my family. Let's stop here, there are nicer memories. And better things to talk about."

# 39

Even Helen's husband was unhappy about her righteous outburst. He put his arm around her to calm her, and tried to explain. "In an emergency, and there was an emergency at that time, the rules change. If you see that a guy is going to attack me, I am sure you will do anything in your power to prevent that, even if it means harming the guy. If a guy tries to rape you I don't mind shooting him to keep him from raping you. The rules change."

Her father also started to take part. "Some day I will tell you about my experiences in Korea. Look at the poor people in North Korea under Communist rule behind barbed wire. Or how many Germans have died trying to escape the East German Communists. Your ideals are high and I am proud of you, but you have to also learn about reality. I think we should talk about it some other time."

I suggested another cup of coffee to get the conversation changed, and then continued.

"The time to leave Germany was rapidly approaching for us. Due to the nature of my work I was exposing my family to grave danger and Margo had already gone through two attempts to

Horst Schneider

have her kidnapped, which was one way to force certain husbands to follow across the border to the Communist East Germany.

Getting to immigrate to the US was no easy matter in the nineteen fifties. First there was the matter of a quota, and then you had to have a sponsor who would guarantee that the immigrants would not become a financial burden to the government.

Sure, we knew quite a few Americans at the time, but none had the financial standing to qualify as a sponsor. Fortunately, my work in US intelligence helped us to bypass the quota problem. The quota we got in no time.

There was no question where to live in the US. While a POW in Colorado Springs I had fallen in love with that place. So I decided to write a letter to the city's mayor with the request of forwarding my letter to the local newspaper.

The mayor's office did that and the Colorado Springs Gazette published a short article quoting our letter. In the letter I had explained my desire to immigrate and that I was trying to find a sponsor. We received two replies from families who offered support but could not sponsor us, again because of their financial standings.

But before I even knew that my letter had actually reached the newspaper I was called into headquarters where a Colonel Colpin started to question me as to how I came to know a certain Mr. Bonforte. I had never heard this name before, but soon learned from Col. Colpin that John Bonforte was a Navy Lt. Commander, Rtd., now a well-known Colorado Springs businessman, and that he had inquired about me through official Pentagon channels. The puzzle fell into place and I was able to give the Colonel a satisfactory explanation.

A short time later John Bonforte wrote us a letter offering to be our sponsor, provided we would pay our own way. He even asked a friend, the president of the Arkansas Valley Bank in Pueblo, to look us over while vacationing in Europe, which he did. All answers must have been positive, because we received the coveted sponsor's papers in the mail shortly after his friend's visit. We were a giant step closer to our goal.

Applications were sent to the US Consulate in Frankfurt and we soon received our expedited quota number and, after some more correspondence, we sent our health certificates to the consulate. We did not have long to wait before we were instructed to present ourselves at the Consulate to be sworn in. The Consul was a lady, and after some preliminary questions she asked us to rise and raise our right hand.

It was an emotional moment, the last step before our goal, the immigration papers. The lady Consul raised her right hand and started the oath, which we repeated after her. She still had in front of her our dossier at which she was looking while administering the oath, and then she suddenly stopped in the middle of the sentence.

'I see here that you were in the US before and that you had a 'Secret' clearance, is that true?'

'Yes, madam,' I answered, somewhat perplexed. And then the sky fell in on us with her next announcement.

'I am sorry,' she explained, 'but I will need an FBI clearance before I can swear you in and give you your immigration visa.' We were stunned as we left the Consulate. Margo was weeping frustrated tears and I had a tough time consoling her. But as so often in our lives, the apparent hurdle turned out to be a blessing.

We had hoped to have enough money for the fare by the time we received our visa, but as it turned out we were woefully short.

For a number of reasons we had elected to use the Holland America Line, which meant that we had to pay our passage with US dollars. This posed somewhat of a problem for us since the possession of US currency was illegal at the time. But we found a way to bypass that dilemma.

To change my German marks into US military script money I first had to dicker with some shady figures standing in darkened doorways at night. I was lucky not to get arrested, because the possession of military script would have brought a stiff jail sentence.

Then I had to ask my American friends to get me US traveler's checks in exchange for the military script. Every step was illegal and fraught with danger. The specter of several years in jail was my constant companion.

The additional time we now had, allowed us to accumulate more money, especially since Margo was highly successful in her job as a department store demonstrator of the then new gold anodized aluminum costume jewelry.

For Margo that meant getting up early before sunrise, hiking to the train station, riding the train to the city of Worms, and then standing all day behind her display just inside the department store entrance, demonstrating and selling her wares. And I must confess, she made considerably more money than I, the so-called breadwinner.

I think I better stop at this point and tell you a story that is so unbelievable that we have hardly ever told it to anyone. I believe that in our family only our son ever heard this story. But it is a true story. Even we could not quite believe it when it happened.

But before I go on I think I would like to wet my tongue with a few sips of Irish Cream. My glass has been empty for much too long."

We chatted for a few minutes while I sipped on my Irish Cream. When my glass was down to half full I went on.

# 40

"This unusual story had its start in Mannheim in the summer of 1953, one year before we left for America.

It was late afternoon one day when I entered a small café on the main drag. The café was empty, except for one lone customer sitting in a corner in the back of me. I had just lit a cigarette, put some sugar in my cup, and poured coffee from the silver coffee carafe when the lady behind me shouted 'Hans'. After she called again 'Hans', I was wondering if she meant me since there was no one else in the café.

As I turned I looked straight into the highly excited and angry face of the young lady behind me who bore an uncanny resemblance to Margo.

A lively conversation followed, during which she accused me of breaking my promise, of abandoning her, and more of the same. Eventually it dawned on me to me that she mistook me for her fiancée who had disappeared during the war.

I tried hard to convince her that I was not her 'Hans' as she thought. But I was not successful, she refused to believe me.

'I recognized you immediately when you came in,' she said, 'and I watched you sit down the way you always did. Why deny it. The way you light your cigarette, the way you carefully prepare your coffee, the way you move, all that gives you away'.

I finally left her with my promise to meet her at the café again the following week, and even bring my wife with me. And I wondered if she believed me that I would come back.

As Margo and I entered the café a week later she greeted us with a strange expression on her face as she looked at Margo. It was a shock for us, too. Those two looked like two sisters. She then introduced herself, her name was Marlene. We had a long and a much more pleasant conversation, which ended with her inviting us to her apartment.

It was there that Margo and I had another shock. Marlene showed us some photos of her Hans and as I looked at them in disbelief I was staring at myself. A very strange and disconcerting experience indeed. Here I stood next to two look-alike ladies, whose names, Margo and Marlene, were even similar. And as I looked at the photos I saw myself standing in places I had never been in my life.

Our encounter soon developed into a nice friendship. And it turned out to be a great blessing. Marlene was a department store demonstrator for the then brand new costume jewelry made of gold anodized aluminum. She was the one who was instrumental in Margo getting the same kind of job in a department store in Worms. She lied to the regional supervisor, telling him that she had worked with Margo before, and how good she was.

What a lucky meeting in this Mannheim café had been became clear very soon. As I told you a while ago, Margo was so good at her sales job that she wound up making much more money than I brought home. And without that extra money we would not have been able to afford our passage to America until much later.

You may call it spooky, you may call it a coincidence, or you may call it Karma, or whatever, call it what you will."

I paused to let the impact of this crazy story sink in, and also to get myself back on an even keel, because even today, this incident makes me feel a bit strange. But then I went on.

"Just before our departure, when Margo was supposed to turn over her inventory to the newly hired demonstrator, she became ill. So much so that she was unable to get out of bed to go to Worms. This job then fell to me.

I bravely embarked on this venture and took the train to Worms. Naturally, no one in the department store knew me and I could just imagine the difficulty of getting the merchandise out of storage and getting the displays set up. Fortunately this was Germany. And knowing how Germans reacted to authority, or at least to perceived authority, I took the elevator to the top floor, which was the storage area.

There I just took control, acting as if I was in charge, commandeering workers and directing traffic. It worked out beautifully; the doors to the storage area were unlocked and everyone hustled to comply with my orders. In the USA I surely would have been challenged as to my authority, but this was Germany in 1954.

When the time came to pay our fare we were still short but were able to get a loan, which we repaid as soon as I started working at the Broadmoor Hotel in Colorado Springs. It called for a lot of belt tightening and scrimping, And the next time we presented ourselves at the US Consulate we were sworn in without a hitch."

Here Margo interrupted. 'Don't you think it is time to stop for today and have dinner,' she asked me, noticing that I was getting a bit tired, and I wholeheartedly agreed. But then I changed my mind. Let's hang on just a few minutes. Until we leave Europe I said to myself.

"Give them just a few minutes so we can leave Europe," I told Margo. "I have my reasons for that, OK?" She smiled back at me and nodded, she obviously understood.

"One of the reasons we left Germany via Holland was that leaving via a German port would have meant a forced 24-hour quarantine, which we could not afford, since there was still a silly tax liability on the books.

About two months prior to our departure Margo was called in to the Revenue Office for Self-employed. Since it was January or February she wore her fur coat, to which a number of rabbits had contributed. At the Revenue Office she was informed that she had been assessed a substantial income tax.

Our magazine business had been a flop and we had finally given it up around Christmas the year before, in 1953. It had been in her name for certain reasons and they claimed that she must have made more profit than she had claimed, after all, she obviously had made a good living. How else could she afford a fur coat, she was told. She tried to explain that it was not a mink, but a rabbit coat. But that didn't get her anyplace.

Her explanation that her husband had a well paying job did not help either. They told her, here we deal only with the self-employed, his records are with the Office for Salaried and we have nothing to do with that office. And since she did not pay that crazy tax they sent the sheriff to attach our property.

Fortunately this was not too long before our departure and the sheriff, who knew our financial situation, was able to procrastinate. In fact, Margo told him the date when we would leave, and he promised to wait until the day after our departure to cart off our typewriter etc. In a letter from our old landlord we heard later that the sheriff had kept his promise."

Now Margo was determined to have me quit for the day and go someplace for a nice relaxing dinner. "If any of you have any more questions you will have to wait till I am sitting comfortably at a table with my Brandy Alexander in my hand," she almost shouted. "I don't know about any of you but I am hungry."

The Lady had spoken, and that was that.

Needless to say, we had a nice dinner, after all, it was our friends' treat. Naturally, there were still quite a few more questions, but I told them that for today I had closed shop.

Our friends finally agreed that I had talked enough for the day. We finished our dinner and drained the last drops from our glasses. As we said good-bye they added a promise, or maybe it was a threat, to return the next day, Sunday, about three. We knew that the Sunday session could not go on too long since Bill's son and wife had tickets on the evening plane.

# 41

# AMERICA!!!

"I think we will now switch from Europe to America," I told them after we had seated ourselves comfortably around our living room. "This then is our third life as I have mentioned to you on Friday.

Our ship was the Ryndam of the Holland America Line. We embarked in Rotterdam on March 19, and we had a very pleasant trip until we left Ireland and hit the Atlantic. Margo and I were dancing after dinner when suddenly the ship lurched and dancers, glasses, and even the dance band, found themselves in a corner of the dance floor. From then on we battled a ferocious storm. It was so bad that the ship was forced to make an unscheduled port call in Halifax for a day.

We started to worry because this put us behind by two days and we were afraid that we might not make the deadline for arrival according to our visa. As it turned out we made it in time on the last day just before our visa expired on March 29, 1954.

Arriving in New York harbor and sailing past the Statue of Liberty was an undescribable, most emotional feeling, a feeling that is impossible to describe in words. Many tears were shed that day, by us, as well as by many other passengers, as we sailed past the lady who promised a new beginning.

I stopped here for a few moments. Margo reached out her hand to touch mine. We sat there for a few seconds till I could go on.

"When we arrived in Hoboken there was a dock strike going on and no tug boats were available, however, the captain of the Ryndam berthed the ship expertly at the pier by using the ship's own power. Even we passengers helped by handling some of the hawsers. Maybe this was an omen: better be prepared to do yourself what you have to do and not rely on others.

We stayed in New York for two days with the family of a GI who we had met in Mannheim one night. He had partied with friends and was much too tipsy to get to his base. We had put him up for the night at our apartment, so he would not get into trouble with a roving military patrol.

When we left New York our friends took us to the bus station and offered us two paper grocery sacks with fruit and candy and cookies for the trip. We were too proud to tell them that we had only 17 cents in our pocket at the time. They probably would have forced ten bags of food on us. The cookies and fruit lasted two days and were very much appreciated.

But we finally ran out of food somewhere in Kansas. About that time a lady was getting ready to get off the bus. And as she passed our seats she remarked about the kids being so well behaved and then she asked us if we were immigrants. When we said, yes, indeed we were, she got three dollar bills out of her handbag and handed each of the kids a dollar bill for good luck as she left. We did not have to go hungry after all.

The three days on the bus from New York to Denver are a blur in my memory. All of us were glued to the window to see what the country looked like, which was to be our home.

But every once in a while we wondered. Had we made the right decision? We wanted desperately to give our kids the chance to be free. Free of the shackles of the old continent. But was this really the Land of the Free? Or had we been fooled? Only the future could tell.

As I told you yesterday, we had written a letter to the mayor of Colorado Springs, and that we had received two offers of assistance should we come to the States.

One of the two couples who had written us in response to our letter was Gene and Dorcas MacAllister. They even offered to take us in for a few days once we arrived. I am ashamed to admit it, but I have forgotten the name of the other couple who wrote to us, except that his name was Bob.

In 1954 there was still a wartime travel tax of 10% in effect. But we saved that 10% tax when a friend of ours offered to buy the bus tickets in Paris where he had to go the following week.

We had expected to continue with Greyhound all the way through to Colorado Springs. But Gene MacAllister had other ideas, he decided to meet us in Denver.

Everybody left the bus when we arrived in Denver to stretch their legs and walk around in the terminal. I had gone to the Greyhound counter for some reason, leaving Margo and the kids behind. She was quite startled when a stranger approached her and started to talk to her in English. Naturally, she didn't understand one word, besides her own name. It was Gene who had spotted her and had recognized her from a picture of us we had sent him.

What a memorable drive south to Colorado Springs it we had. I can still feel the excitement when I first spotted the castle on top of Castle Rock, and the awe at the awesome sights in the Garden of the Gods through which Gene MacAllister drove us on the way to his house in Manitou Springs.

And I will never forget the first dinner Dorcas served us as a welcome dinner. It was roast duck with sweet potatoes, sweet corn, and Jell-O with carrots and celery.

My God, whoever heard of Jell-O with vegetables in Germany? And even worse, there were sweet potatoes. The only potatoes known in Germany at that time that were sweet, were potatoes which froze in the cellar and should have been thrown away.

The corn was excellent, but it brought back memories. After the war the US shipped tons and tons of food to starving Germany, among which was canned sweet corn. But the only corn known then in Europe was chicken feed corn. And so, instead of being thankful, we Germans felt the victors were making fun of the vanquished by sending them chicken feed to eat. Today we laugh about such misunderstandings.

Once in a while we stole a glance at the kids who answered us with sour looks that said, how can you eat this stuff. But eat it they did. And when one of the MacAllisters looked their way, they were all smiles and happy, as if this was the best dinner of their lives."

"They sound like a wonderful couple to know. You were lucky to run into friends like Gene and Dorcas when you came to the US. I am sure you stayed in touch with them. Where are they now?" It was Helen who sounded very happy we had a good beginning in America.

"The news is not all that good, Helen," I informed her. "Shortly after our arrival they got a divorce and shortly thereafter she had to be committed to an institution. We had noticed already before their separation that she was rather unstable. Gene was devastated and went downhill from there. His personality changed. There were times when he was almost like the old Gene we knew, but most of the time he was just not the same. We later on heard that he had died in Morrison, near Denver.

# 42

We did not meet our sponsors, John Bonforte and his wife, until about a month after we had arrived. We first wanted to get on our feet financially before meeting them so as not to create the impression that we were in need of their assistance. They were fiercely independent, and so were we.

But finding a job was not an easy task, and I needed a job now, maybe tomorrow, but not next month. I tried the local High School, after all I could teach math, or physics, or chemistry. There I found out that to be a teacher in the US did not depend on the mastery of the subject matter but on the possession of a teacher's certificate.

They gave me hope, though. They arranged for an interview with the head of the Chemistry Department at the college. He was most gracious, and after a lengthy interview indeed offered me a teaching job, although only part time, starting next semester. This was too late for me, and the salary would have been less than what I needed.

I was getting desperate. At the old Antlers Hotel I had been turned down again, and as I was walking along I stopped in at the Manhattan Broiler, a local pub, and I hit pay dirt. They needed a dishwasher badly.

I jumped at the chance, After all, what was more natural for an immigrant than to start life in the US washing dishes for a living! This job meant a lengthy bus ride to town at noon and a one-hour walk home at night. And it was a smelly, dirty job.

Both Gene MacAllister as well as Bob, whose last name I can't recall, kept scouting around for a job for me. Bob had a relative who was headwaiter at the Tavern at the Broadmoor Hotel. One day Bob called to tell me about an opening as a waiter at the Broadmoor. He asked me if I had had some experience in that field. Certainly, I told him, I had some experience. I had waited on tables while in college, I told him, which was a blatant lie. But it got me the job, which was a vast improvement over washing dishes at the Manhattan Broiler.

For three and a half years I worked at the Broadmoor, six days a week, from eleven in the morning till after midnight. The pay was 46 cents a day, out of which I had to pay the hotel for the cost of my uniform and for uniform laundry; it was the tips that counted. The first night I came home utterly exhausted but exuberant, telling Margo that here we would get rich, hadn't I made six dollars in tips today?

It was only after I had started work as a waiter at the Broadmoor Hotel that we placed a phone call to the Bonfortes. Mrs. Bonforte answered the phone, and when I explained that we had just recently arrived from Germany she asked that we please arrive at their home about six PM.

We were greeted cordially when we arrived and

were asked to join the rest of the delegation. This was a surprise to us, we had expected to meet just the Bonfortes. It turned out that there was also a delegation of German teachers traveling the US who had been invited by the Bonfortes for dinner that evening.

Dinner was to be on top of Cheyenne Mountain, and after the obligatory cocktails had been consumed we all piled into waiting cars. Mrs. Bonforte came over to us and invited us to join her for the drive in her private Cadillac.

At the Cheyenne Mountain Lodge Margo was asked to sit to the right of Mr. Bonforte, and I was placed to the right of Mrs. Bonforte, and the dinner was served.

The dinner was excellent, a connoisseur obviously had selected the wine, and the conversation was interesting and lively. Finally Mrs. Bonforte asked me where we were from, and when I told her, she was surprised to meet people from the same city as the couple they were sponsoring. And she was even more amazed when it turned out that we were indeed that couple.

She later told us that she had thought we were part of the German teachers delegation. But she had taken a liking to us right from the start, and that was why we were invited to ride in her car, and why we were placed at the table as guests of honor.

Our life has been full of such coincidences. Another one occurred one evening at the Broadmoor. It was a slow evening with little to do until the captain finally seated a middle-aged couple in my station.

During the meal the gentleman asked me my name and where I came from, and then commented on the unusual fact that he happened to know of someone by the same name in the same city in Germany. I had to agree that that was rather unusual.

A bit later, after dinner, he introduced himself as Gen. Chidlaw, Commander of US Air Defense Command in Cheyenne Mountain. It was then that I put two and two together and asked him if he ever had heard of 'Rustavi'.

He had a very strange look on his face when he next wanted to know what I knew about 'Rustavi'. And when I told him that I was the one who had originated the report about the secret installation near that city in Russia, he jumped up and pumped my hand.

'I have to do something about you, you don't belong here,' he said and invited me to his HQ downtown next Monday. To make a long story short, he offered me to run the new computer they were installing, a Univac. But he could not help me either, this was a government job and the position required US citizenship.

# 43

The nineteen fifties were a time of feverish prospecting for uranium in the western states such as Utah and Colorado. One day I waited on a gentleman who was the editor of a publication, 'The Mining Record'. He invited me to write an article for his paper about uranium mining in Germany. He published my short article and paid me 50 dollars for my effort, a princely sum of money then. But more important, this almost turned out to be a turning point in my life.

The president of a Colorado Springs company, 'Atomic Research Corp.', read my article. He inquired at the Mining Record and found out that I worked at the Broadmoor Hotel. There he looked me up and invited me to appear as his guest on his TV show the next evening.

Shortly thereafter he offered me a job as his chief chemist. But it shouldn't be. The uranium boom turned into a bust just at that time and "Atomic Research' went under with it.

I had one more chance to escape waiting on tables when I was offered a research job dealing with a sea water desalination process. This also ended after a few weeks and I was back at the Broadmoor as a waiter.

But working as a waiter at the Broadmoor for four years was enough for me, and I started to look for a change of scenery.

My new job also was a waiter's job, but it was so different from the job at the Broadmoor.

The Garden Of The Gods Club was upscale, and it was a fun place to work. The scenery was absolutely fantastic. There I volunteered to work breakfast, lunch, and dinner. Off I would go in the morning to start work at seven, then I would take a break after lunch from three till five.

Often my sweetheart picked me up after lunch and we would drive into the Garden of the Gods where I could crash on a blanket for an hour and a half before going back on the floor till after midnight. Yes, the hours were long, but the tips were good.

I said it was fun to work there and I have many funny stories that I tell once in a while. Remind me some day to tell you some of the funnier ones. But today I will tell you just one story, which illustrates why it was enjoyable to work there.

The clientele consisted of people born into money, and these people are easy to wait on. There was the owner, for instance, the oil magnate Hill from Texas. He sometimes would come in for breakfast and afterwards grab me by the arm and drag me, still in my waiters uniform, to the greens for some putting practice. And I still don't care for golf.

But I wanted to tell you a little story. We sometimes had a group of ladies coming in for an afternoon cocktail party. When that happened I stayed on all afternoon, after all the tips were good. And if the majority of the ladies were guests of the Club for the first time, the hostess would often pass by me, and with a conspiratorial wink, whisper to me, 'Henry'. That was my cue for a little fun.

Once everyone had their first drink I would wait for just the right moment to start my spiel. I would walk around the table as usual, with my hands behind my back. And every now and then I would steal a quick surreptitious glance under the table. It never was long before one of the ladies would ask me if anything was wrong.

'Oh no,' I would answer, 'nothing is wrong.' A few more glances under the table and now they really had to know what the problem was, to which I would answer with 'Nothing really wrong, madam. It is only that I am concerned.' Now this always piqued their curiosity.

Their next question 'Concerned about what, sir?' was what I had been waiting for.

'I am concerned about Henry,' I would answer with a straight face. 'He has a lame leg. He is our pet mouse.'

The more of her guests fell for this charade, the better my tip was later. And if one or more shrieked, my tip doubled.

But the Garden of the Gods Club was open only during the summer and I knew I had to look for another job again soon. But it had been a fun job, nevertheless.

# 44

Certainly a million times better than the first one I had had, where I worked in a steamy, smelly, and dingy cubicle among dirty dishes, garbage, and smelly wet towels. But as always, there was a redeeming moment. It taught me something important about my new country.

The place I am talking about was the Manhattan Broiler near the old Antler's Hotel.

One evening an absolutely huge black man walked into my place, almost filling what little free space there was. He looked me over for a while and then asked if I had been a soldier in the German forces. When I nodded my head, not knowing what he was after, he raised his right arm towards me and showed me a pair of shiny steel tongs where his hand had been.

'Any idea,' he asked rhetorically, 'who did this? It was some Kraut who maybe didn't like my black face.'

I had already retreated as far as I could, there was no place to go, and I could already see myself in a bloody heap on the floor.

He stepped even closer and I could hardly believe

his next words. 'You guys fought for your country as we did for ours, and now that you are here you will be you of ours and we better have a drink on that.'

A drink we had, the owner even paid for it, and this was one of the best welcomes I had had in my life.

# 45

Another memorable welcome happened not very long afterwards. This also happened during one of the first days after our arrival in Colorado Springs.

One sunny day we strolled along Ute Ave. past a used car dealership and the owner of the business started to give us a sales pitch as we passed. We explained to him that a car was not yet on our agenda, since we had only recently arrived from Germany. Other items were much more necessary right now, such as pots and pans, etc.

At this his eyes lit up and he told us that he recently had run a special promotion, giving away a set of cookware to any newlyweds buying a car from him. And it so happened, he said, that he still had one set left. And he couldn't think of anyone more in need than we, and please, accept this as my gift to you for coming to America.

This dealership is long gone, but the memories linger. And even today, after forty-six years, we are still using two of those first pots in our kitchen.

There was no question in our mind as to where we would buy our first car.

Only a short time after I had started to work at the

Broadmoor Hotel I was back at that dealership. And soon I found myself sitting in a black 1937 Chrysler sedan that was to become our very first car. I had told the dealer that my international driver's license was still in some luggage that had not arrived yet. This seemed to satisfy him, because he went back to his office to finish his paperwork.

Naturally, you realize, don't you, that I did not have any kind of driver's license. So I was now sitting in the car trying to figure out the gear shift arrangement, and which pedal was the accelerator, which was the brake, and which was the clutch.

By a strange coincidence we had exactly fifty dollars to our name, the exact price of the car. When the owner found that out he gave me back fifty cents so I could buy two gallons of gasoline. We were broke again, but we were happy, we were in America, I had a job, and now we even had a car.

Getting our first car called for something special, like driving downtown to visit our friend Bob who had a small business in downtown Colorado Springs.

The street where he was located had angle parking and was crowned much more than normal. Had we arrived from the east we could have easily pulled into the one empty parking spot in front of his place. But this being our first drive in our first car, Murphy's Law dictated that we arrive driving on the opposite side of the street.

It would not have been a problem with today's cars, but that old 1937 Chrysler had a much larger turning radius than expected, certainly much larger than I had expected.

And so I turned and then found myself looking at the back end of the car next to the empty parking slot. That was no great problem, I thought, all I had to do was back up and then drive forward again.

As I said before, the street had a vicious crown, and every time I released the clutch the car wanted to roll forward unless I stepped on the brake. If I released the brake and the clutch both to put my foot on the gas pedal, the car stalled.

There was only one way to solve that problem. I asked Margo to reach for the wheel, while I ducked under the dash. Now my feet could operate the clutch pedal and the brake pedal at the same time while with my right hand I could operate the gas pedal.

I recall that there was some horn honking, and I am sure that there was also some head scratching, after all, how often do you see a car driving backwards and then forward without a driver at the wheel.

# 46

It was less than a year after we had arrived in Colorado Springs that Margo decided to drive her car to the school to pick up the kids. This was to be the surprise of surprises for the kids, and she could already in her mind's eye visualize their smiles. It was Mother's first drive without a chaperone and Margo knew that the kids would be very proud of her. However, her drive almost turned out different.

Margo was still learning English. As she approached the school, she saw a sign and tried to read it, but by the time she understood what it said she was already past it. She was lucky that day, the police car monitoring the traffic in front of the school was just then driving off. They say that kids born on a Sunday are lucky and Margo seemed to prove that the old adage was right.

Margo had passed her drivers license test only a week before she ventured out on her own to drive to the school. Her English was still in its infancy, especially her reading. She tried hard, but English spelling being as crazy as it is, it was tough on her. You cannot really sound out a word, it often looks so different on paper than it sounds. It had been just a week before that she had asked me how to pronounce the word l-a-u-g-h. I told her but she thought I had misunderstood her and so asked me again, spelling it out l-a-u-g-h. To my answer she replied, 'how can it be if it is spelled l-a-u-g-h?' I could only whole-heartedly agree with her. That had made her wonder how she could possibly pass her driver's test. But she was a spunky girl and we ventured forth to try it anyway. On her written test she struggled mightily and even answered many questions correctly, but she could not answer an even greater number of questions because she did not understand them.

At this point I stepped in and told the examiner what the problem was. He was willing to rephrase the questions into simpler English and administer the test verbally. Now Margo sailed right through without a hitch. Then she also sailed through her driving test and finally an ecstatic Margo received her coveted license. She should have sent that examiner a bouquet of roses.

It was only natural that Margo wanted to contribute financially, and as soon as she felt that she knew enough English to get by, she went to Sears Roebuck and applied for employment. She would pester the poor employment clerk week after week until finally, probably out of sheer frustration, she was hired as a sales clerk.

As time went by she learned that what she sold in millinery was not spelled 'head', but 'hat'. This and other little blunders kept the back office in stitches, and even up front on the floor she inadvertently created amusing situations.

One such occurred one day when an old farmer

asked for drawers for his wife. The sales girls, naturally, sent him to Margo and then stood back to watch as poor Margo was trying to send him to the furniture department. The farmer then tried another tack and asked for a pair of ham bags. Margo had never heard of ham bags and now suggested he go to the house wares department.

Now the farmer became agitated and insisted that he was in the right place, and after some more argument, the girls finally stepped in and sold him the panties for his wife he had asked for.

Later she was transferred to the cosmetics department, which was much more to her liking. There she came into her own and, after a short time, was promoted to assistant department manager with an increase in salary.

This new position not only brought her an increased paycheck, but she also received a percentage of sales of certain beauty lines that were assigned to her. Being persistent and stubborn had finally paid off, although Margo never admitted to being stubborn, - she called it 'determined'.

# 47

Our relationship with Sears, Roebuck actually had started earlier, almost right after we arrived in Colorado Springs. Since we needed so many things, such as blankets, dishes, etc., it was only natural to turn to a large retailer such as Sears.

And so I visited Sears and asked the girl in the outer office to let me speak to the manager. Instead of announcing me to the manager, she wanted to know what I wanted from him. I finally answered: 'I would have asked for you if I wanted to tell you my troubles.'

This conversation seemed to have piqued his curiosity, because he stuck his head through the door to see who I was and I brazenly walked in and told him: 'I am an immigrant who has just arrived and I need credit in the worst way. Obviously, I have no credit rating.'

At this he raised his hands as if to say no, but I stubbornly continued: 'I am not up on American history but there must have been a Mr. Sears and a Mr. Roebuck. They did not have all the modern conveniences you have today to check up on a person. Instead they looked that person in the eye and then

Horst Schneider

made their decision. They were so successful at that that their business grew to the point where they had to appoint managers like you to continue. Today you are given the opportunity to prove that you are worthy your appointment. Can you do it?'

He hesitated only a short moment before he got up, walked around his desk, put his hands on my shoulder and smilingly said: 'I think you will make it in this country.' And with that we had our credit.

Our first apartment in Colorado Springs was located in the Mexican quarter, in the rear of a duplex in the basement. It was a one and a half room apartment, with a tiny living room, a small kitchenette and the kids' 'room', which actually was a like a large walk-in closet. There was not enough room even in the living room for a decent table.

We had a bunk bed for the three kids, the two girls sharing the lower bed, and Dieter sleeping upstairs. Margo and I slept on the convertible couch, which besides a chair, was the only furniture in the living room. But there was one more item in the living room, a big black and white television set, the gift from a neighbor. This TV ran day and night, and it helped Margo learn English

The furniture we bought on time payments from American Furniture, where we established credit the same way we had established credit at Sears. After all, it worked fine once, why not a second time. The apartment may not have looked like the Taj Majal but it had a floor on which one could walk barefoot without getting splinters. And it had two wonderful luxuries we had not had all these years in Schimmeldewog or in Mannheim. There was hot running water right from the faucet, and it also had a shower.

The one table we owned was in the kitchen. It was cramped quarters when Margo was cooking and the three kids were trying to do their homework. But that meant little to us, we smelled the future and the future smelled good.

"That must have been terribly cramped," said Helen, "I don't believe I could have done that. We live in a three bedroom house with a double garage and still don't have enough room, I don't see how you managed. How long did you live there?"

"We lived in that apartment about one year before we had enough money to move to a two bed room apartment upstairs. There the kids finally had their own room," I answered her.

"Next door to us, in the other down stairs duplex apartment, lived a divorced Mexican lady with a little boy and one girl. The girl's name was LaVerne. She was about Sigrid's age, somewhere around ten years old. It was her job to tend to her brother while mother was gone to work most evenings.

Many afternoons Laverne could be found in our apartment jabbering away at Margo. She had taken a great liking to Margo and had started to teach Margo the English names of whatever there was in the kitchen. And she seemed to have been a good teacher, because Margo picked up English in amazingly short time.

LaVerne also enjoyed working with Margo around the kitchen, such as helping with the dishes, or doing general cleanup. And after the chores were done the two would play with a set of pick-up sticks, which was one of the little girl's greatest joys. I guess Margo was some sort of mother substitute to LaVerne.

# 48

There were several neighbors who had heard about this immigrant couple that had moved in. Maybe it was through their kids, I presume. At any rate, Margo wound up with clothes for our kids, a radio, an electric iron, a toaster, and various other items for the household.

At first she tried to refuse, which was the right thing to do according to the old German ways, but she was told that now she was in America, and that is the way we do things here. We help those who need help.

In this way she became acquainted with some of our neighbors, Ruby especially, who lived three houses east of us and also had three kids, slightly older than ours. Several times Margo was asked by Ruby to come and visit until Ruby finally told her to either come and visit or she wouldn't come to see Margo any more.

Margo's problem was that the invitation was done so casually, not as formal as she was used to in Germany. Therefore Margo considered it to be only a warm and polite, but meaningless gesture.

And now that Margo knew she had to go and visit Ruby at her home she wanted to know on what day and at what time. Ruby, not knowing the ways of the old country, told her something like 'how about later this week, maybe about three or four.' And it was not until Margo had pinned her down to a certain day, and the exact time, that the two finally got together.

This was one of the first new customs she came across, and it was also her very first acquaintance with the more casual American approach to life. In the old country one would never have been given a time like 'three or four'.

I remember an invitation to a party given by an American couple in Mannheim who invited their German guests to come at 'about five to six'. The result was that about half of the German guests showed up exactly at five, the rest of the guests arrived punctually at six.

About this time our youngest daughter Doris, five years old at the time, was given a kitten, our first member of the Schneider Zoo. But it was not long before the kitten had company. One day Margo saw a black dog in the back yard, limping along, holding his front paw off the ground. After she finally had him coaxed close she was able to remove the clump of burrs from his front paw. That's how and why Blackie adopted his new owner.

Margo kept telling me what a loyal and sweet dog he was and how she would like to adopt him. I told her that he might be sweet but we didn't know where he came from, what diseases he might harbor, that we would be financially responsible if he bit someone, etc.

The last thing I wanted at that stage in our life was a dog. I pointed out to Margo that (1) we could not afford a dog, that (2) we already had a cat, that (3) he was probably someone else's pet, and that (4) it violated our apartment lease, and that (5) he might harbor fleas, and that (6) I was against it.

I did not know that every morning after I left for work a black dog sneaked into the apartment where he stayed all day with his new master. Then, shortly after midnight, his new master shooed out. The new master would then go to bed pretending to sleep when I came home. But fate is fickle.

One night I returned from work while it was raining hard, and it was cold. Sitting next to our door was this poor black dog, wet, miserable, and shivering. I took pity on the poor creature and let him in. When I asked Margo if it was OK with her she magnanimously agreed to let the dog stay that night. Maybe that is why they say 'It's raining cats and dogs'.

From there the Schneider Zoo expanded to assorted dogs, more kittens, several fleas who enjoyed a meal of my blood before being dispatched, a horned toad, a wild box turtle, and several baby sparrows.

The sparrows arrived while we were living in Denver. Dieter had rescued them from certain death, and then proceeded to rear them with cooked rice. They lived in his room until they were old enough to fly and were then allowed to leave and return through his open window.

He even showed them by example how to pick for seeds, but to the best of my knowledge they learned to fly on their own without Dieter demonstrating the techniques. He was a busy guy while he was mother to his six sparrows. In the house he constantly carried with him a Kleenex tissue, which he needed to clean up the droppings of his charges.

And to his credit it must be stated that he lost only one of his brood. This one came to a premature death one evening while all six birds were cavorting around the living room. We had an unexpected blackout and just as the light went out Sigrid opened the door to her room, the cat got out, and then there were only five.

# 49

But I am getting ahead of my story. We lived in this basement apartment for quite a while until one of the two ground level apartments facing the street became available. There was now more space and each of the kids could have their own bed, and we finally could have our own bedroom.

The next move was to Stratten Meadows, a southern suburb of Colorado Springs. There we bought a three-bedroom tract house. Margo at last had a real kitchen and the girls had their own room.

When we had bought our first car, we had had just barely enough money saved to buy it. Now again we had just barely enough money saved to buy our castle. After we signed the papers it was time to pay. That's when there were some eyebrows raised by a stuffy real estate broker and also by an even stuffier lawyer.

There was also a lady typist present. She almost choked on suppressed laughter as we laid out first the paper money, then stacked up the half-dollars, the quarters and finally the dimes and the nickels. We just had enough money for the down payment, and that was it. All we had left in our pockets was a little change. Today we chuckle and find the whole thing hilarious but at the time there was nothing funny about it.

Sally burst out, "you actually bought a house and paid with nickels and dimes? That takes the cake. You never told us about that and I think it's one of the funniest stories I heard from you. No wonder those guys raised their eyebrows and the typist almost choked."

Her husband also had to say something. "Horst," he said, "you should have considered becoming a professional gambler. But, yes, I can see it in my mind's eye, you two sitting there calmly stacking up the coins as if this was the way one normally buys a house."

The laughter finally died down and I could continue.

"Eventually we even bought some more furniture. But much of the furniture we made ourselves.

In Colorado Springs was a lumberyard, which had a mountain of scrap plywood pieces, many of them birch, and even walnut and cherry, which they sold for only pennies. Here we bought small and larger pieces for our kid's furniture.

Margo had bought a ¼" drill for me as a birthday gift. It came with a little attachment for a 4" saw blade. This little attachment is still in use today, fifty years later, long after the original drill itself has bitten the dust.

This little saw blade saw a lot of action and soon we had transformed the pieces of plywood into furniture, with the help of stacks of sandpaper, applied with plenty of elbow grease, followed by a good measure of spar varnish. There were three desks, one for each of the kids, as well as some chests of triple drawers. I understand that one of those chests of drawers still exists today, in the year 2000.

I finally decided that I had had enough of working as a waiter and was looking for some alternative. Along came an offer from World Book Encyclopedia to establish myself as a salesman first, with a good chance to later become a district manager. I faithfully attended the training course for several weeks and then hit the streets. But try as I may, there were two aspects I never mastered. While I was rated excellent at doing a presentation I was only fair to poor at closing the deal.

But the most difficult part was knocking on a door cold turkey. I was a miserable failure, and finally I had to admit it to myself. It was a real low time in my life. Luckily, Margo held up her part of the bargain, worked all day, cooked in the evening, and did all the other chores that had to be done while I felt sorry for myself.

But her salary alone could not carry us financially and Margo finally put me back on track. I went back to waiting on tables at the Broadmoor Hotel.

There was just one item Margo claimed she needed to make her happiness complete. It was a carpet for the living room. We spent a whole morning at Sears looking at carpets, finally deciding on the size and on the color. It was not an in-stock item and therefore had to be specially ordered. It was fairly close to Christmas and she hoped that it could be delivered before Christmas. The salesman assured her that that was possible. And with that assurance we left the store.

But she had not reckoned with the deviousness of her husband and her three kids who together conspired against her. We contacted the carpet salesman to make sure that the carpet would be delivered on Christmas Eve but without her knowing about it. He went along with our plan and contacted Margo a little later to tell her the bad news that the carpet was delayed and would not arrive until after Christmas.

Margo almost cried. She had been so looking forward to that carpet. Maybe the carpet was something she needed to make her forget that for all these years since the end of the war there had been only bare wood under her feet. And for many years in Mannheim the floorboards were old, burned, and full of splinters.

On Christmas Eve morning she left to go to work as usual while the kids were still sleeping, or so she thought. But the moment her car drove off the kids were out of bed. The paint cans we had secretly bought and smuggled into the house were opened and the kids took up their stations. Each knew what to do and we went to work cleaning and then painting the kitchen, the living room, the bathroom, and our bedroom.

It was late when Margo came home exhausted after an extremely busy day at work. Husbands by the hundreds bought perfumes for their wives. Women bought cosmetics to get them through the holidays till next year. It was a mad day she told us later at dinnertime.

When she stepped through the door that evening she stopped short and just stood inside the door for a moment. What she saw first was a clean and freshly painted home. And then she saw her precious carpet gracing the living room. She cried many tears of happiness that night.

We had arrived in the United States only two years ago with just seventeen cents to our name. This Christmas we owned two cars and a three-bedroom house. This really was the land of unlimited opportunities.

Yes, all the hardships and sacrifices we had endured were worth it. Now we knew for certain that we would be able to offer our kids a better future in a free country."

# 50

At this point I had to stop and wait for that lump in my throat to go away. Margo noticed and petted my arm. Our friends also noticed the tension and kept quiet. It lasted just a few moments before I could go on.

"It was not until 1958 that I came across an ad for a chemist in the Denver newspaper. I was in Denver the very next day and was hired immediately. For about two months I lived in a small room on East Colfax Ave., working during the day, and in the evenings looking for a house to buy for us that we could afford. I finally located one after I had already looked at 87 houses, it was the 88th house and we bought it.

The company I worked for in Denver was the most prominent supplier to hospitals, nursing homes, and restaurants. But a change happened about two years after I had started when this company bought another company that was in the restaurant supply business and I was offered to head the design department.

Two years later, in 1962, I received a still better offer by a manufacturer of stainless steel commercial kitchen equipment. After seven years with that company, and with many hospital, airline, and restaurant kitchen designs to my credit, it was time to make a change and I resigned.

After I resigned in 1969, we took some time out for ourselves, the last few years had been very stressful. We bought a fifth wheel trailer and bummed around the US for some time.

But first we went back to Europe for a visit, the first time since 1954. This time we were strictly tourists from America. We started out by visiting relatives we had not seen for so many years, then also visited friends.

Before we left for Europe we told everyone that only half of the time in Europe was meant for visits, the other half of our vacation would belong to us alone.

We had decided to first play tourist in Margo's hometown, the old city of Aachen. From Aachen we took the northern route through Belgium to Paris.

As we entered Belgium from Germany Margo informed me that she had taken a water pill at breakfast and it definitely was beginning to work. She looked somewhat pale and strained when she said to me 'I have to get to a restroom SOON.'

But there was no restroom in sight and the nearest town where we could get a room for the night was at least a hundred kilometers away. 'There is only one solution,' I told her, 'do what the Belgian girls do. I will stop and you can select the bushes of your choice.'

This solution did not appeal to her. She was in luck, though, a small hamlet appeared magically past the next curve in the road and we decided to go to the bistro we happened to see in the middle of that little village.

By the time we entered the bistro she was a little shaky. She waited only a few seconds after we sat down at one of the few tables before making a beeline to the door at the far end of the room that had a sign above it, which said 'TOILETTES'.

Now she was really in a hurry and almost ripped the door off its hinges to get inside. There, however, she stopped short for a moment. At the wall she was facing was a five-foot long metal trough, similar to an oversized rain gutter. And standing in front of this trough, relieving themselves, were two gentlemen who turned around to see who was coming in. Being Belgian gentlemen they naturally greeted her with a friendly 'Bon jour, Madame.'

Margo hurriedly retreated to one of the two stalls and went about her business trying to be as quiet as possible. She let out a big sigh when she finally heard the door closing two times. With the two gentlemen gone she mustered her courage and stepped out of her cubicle. But again she was greeted by a male voice with a polite 'Bon jour, Madame.' Unbeknownst to Margo another fellow had entered as the second one had left.

She came back to our table with a little sunburn in her face and told me what had happened, as if I had not seen the comings and goings at the toilet. I had no pity with her, she should not have felt embarrassed, unisex toilets in small towns had been the norm in Europe at the time we had left. So fast we forget.

I think I mentioned to you that we had had to learn new customs etc. when we came to America and this was a classic example.

205

# 51

We had occasion to meet up with another example in Paris.

We always have disliked big hotels, famous restaurants and the like. We prefer to be part of the local scene and small hotels have so much more charm than the big modern ones. The old Anglais-Belgique Hotel in Paris was no exception.

It was only four rooms wide, four stories high, and extended somewhat to the rear to accommodate a total of about twenty guestrooms. When we were there in 1969, the rooms already had been modernized. The hotel had moved the bidet next to the other side of the toilet bowl, which made it possible to install a tiny shower in that corner of the restroom. We very much appreciated having a shower in our room.

Shortly before coming to Paris we had stayed in one of the main hotels in Brussels, the one across from the train station. There we had no shower, but were offered the use of the 'bathroom', which was a real Bath Room, a 'Salle de Bain', with a porcelain bath tub.

To get there I had to call the concierge for help. They dispatched a young lady who led me to the end of the hall, down one flight of stairs into another hallway, around a corner and presto, there it was. Our Paris hotel was a huge improvement compared to the one in Brussels.

We had taken up residence at the Anglais-Belgique for the few days we stayed in Paris that year and were glad we had picked this particular hotel because the next morning we had a little paper wedged under the windshield wiper of our car. The paper was a greeting from the Paris police, called an 'Avis de Contravention', a citation in English.

When we told the concierge about it she asked us to hand it to her and she would handle the situation. The following morning we again found a ticket behind the windshield wiper, and the concierge again said she would take care of it. The third morning she suggested that maybe it was time to move the car.

We were extremely lucky to find a parking space just around the corner. We obviously had kept the ticket because it surfaced recently as we looked through some of our old photos.

The second night in Paris was hot and muggy and we slept on top of our covers, with our pajamas on the floor next to our bed, 'in case of fire' we joked. Since it was rather late when we had come home after our evening in the city we had decided to sleep in and not get up at the crack of dawn.

The next morning there was a knock on our door and I heard a voice in front of our door announcing the arrival of a breakfast tray. I was still groggy with sleep and mumbled something like 'just a moment ma'am', while I swung one leg off the bed. But then I remembered that we were in Europe and said, 'Einen Augenblick, bitte.' By this time I was halfway to the door and it finally dawned on me that we were in France and I said: 'Un moment, s'il vous plaît.'

A moment later I had arrived at the door, unlocked it and opened it. It was the concierge with a nice breakfast tray for us. The aroma of the fresh coffee plus the looks of the fresh croissants awakened me fully and I could answer her, yes, we had had a wonderful and restful night, and yes, we will let you know if we want more coffee, and 'merci bien, Madame.'

I closed the door after her and suddenly realized that neither of us had any clothes on. But what the heck, this was not the prudish US, this was Paris."

Helen's eyes were wide. "Weren't you terribly embarrassed, I mean, I would have died right there."

It was time to educate that young, sheltered lady. "No, I was not embarrassed. You see, Germany is an old country. During the Middle Ages there was no running water, the water came from a cistern, or fountain, which was usually located in the middle of the town.

That's where everyone got their water. This was also the meeting place where all the gossip and news was discussed. It was the most important spot in the village, the TV and newspaper of its day.

It was only natural that each town was trying to outdo their neighbors by having a more elaborate, more beautiful fountain. The fountains sported many statues of saints, angels, Greek gods and goddesses etc. There was much nudity.

So, when you grew up as a kid in Germany you lived with nude statues around you and didn't think of them being obscene, they were as natural looking as you yourself. So what could be wrong with them. Boys knew what girls looked like and vice versa. It didn't warp their mind. That warping came to the US with the Puritans.

Someday you will have to clean house and free yourself from some silly ideas that somebody put into your head. You don't necessarily have to be a rebel like us. But if you believe in a Creator you shouldn't call the Creator's work dirty and obscene. Think about it.

# 52

At any rate we enjoyed ourselves as tourists. But all good things come to an end and when we returned home we began to wonder what we should do next, after all, we needed some kind of income.

Going back to work for someone else did not appeal to me, and also, we wanted some venture that would allow us to work together. We went through the Yellow Pages of the phone book for inspirations, but without much success. Those businesses as jeweler or TV repair required special skills I did not have, other businesses were too dirty, too hot, too cold, at any rate, unappealing to us.

Having a business of our own was not exactly a new idea. We, or rather Margo, had acquired a business earlier, four or five years after we had moved to Denver from Colorado Springs. With two young daughters in the house it was only natural that she became interested in the Girl Scouts. That also meant visits to a nearby hobby and craft store where she was a steady customer.

As I said, she acquired a business and here is how that happened. One evening at dinner she mentioned that the owners of her favorite haunt, the Hobby Hut, wanted to take a family vacation in California and needed someone to tend to the business in their absence. This sounded like fun to Margo and she eagerly accepted the challenge.

Two weeks later the owners returned and were amazed at the increase in sales during those fourteen days they had been gone. They even went as far as suggesting that Margo buy the business from them. That evening, again at dinner, Margo told us again what she had done, how much fun she had had, that she was asked to buy the business, and what she would do if this were her business. She kept prattling on and on through dinner and desert about WHAT IF. When I asked her if she really would like to buy the Hobby Hut she was quite emphatic with her 'Yes', not in the least dreaming that this was possible.

It was not until I went to the phone and called the owners that she realized that I had taken her seriously and she frantically waved her arms while silently hollering 'NO, NO'. But it was too late, I had already arranged a meeting for the next day. I sat down to take stock of our finances and I felt that we could buy the business with a little help from our bank.

And that was how just one week later Margo had indeed acquired a business. It was a good investment in many respects. It turned out to be a forced savings account since every penny earned was reinvested in merchandise. Those pennies came in handy later when the business was sold.

More important probably was the fact that our teenagers, Dieter and Doris, could work here. Sigrid, our oldest, had just married and missed all the fun, and fun it was. They found out that they were respected and appreciated by Margo's customers for their knowledge and their attitude. And work they did, selling behind the counter, handling the cash register, stocking merchandise, taking inventory.

The first Christmas taught us a lesson we had not expected. We were glad that the Christmas rush was over and we could take it easy for a while. With this in mind Dieter and I walked to the store the day after Christmas to leisurely take inventory. But we had not reckoned with Johnny urgently needing more tracks for his train set, Jimmy having an airplane but no fuel for it, and Timmy having been given a twenty-dollar bill in the Christmas card from Grandma.

We entered the store from the rear, turned on the lights, and then were stunned by the sight that greeted us. In front of the store were milling around all the Johnnies, and Jimmies, and Timmies of our suburb. I ran to the phone and hollered 'Help, Help' and hung up to let in the multitudes. It was a mad day, the crowd mobbed us, but the cash register rang, just what a new owner needed.

# 53

For the next Christmas we built an HO train layout for the store window, which we fortunately sold after the holiday. This gave us a chance to build a much better one, complete with a hidden lake and a sunbathing lady on the beach being ogled from behind some trees by two fellows. And a train crossing with a reluctant mule being pulled across by a farmer. And many, many little touches more, so that people came back from time to time to discover something they had missed before.

This train layout was nine feet long and took up most of the kitchen while it was under construction. The kitchen at that time was a real mess, there was Plaster of Paris, paint brushes, oil paint, wires, etc., strewn everywhere. But the railroad was a huge success after it was finished and installed in the store window. And the whole family was glad when the kitchen was a kitchen again.

But no one was more glad than Doris. It was during the railroad construction time that she was sent home early one evening to start the dinner, which was fried chicken that night.

She was almost in tears when we arrived home

for dinner. 'Look', she said, 'my chicken will not brown. I floured the pieces as always, but they won't do it.' Margo finally solved the mystery when she saw the bag with the Plaster of Paris standing next to the stove."

Sally chimed in here, turning to Margo, "working in your store was probably almost a better education than the one they could get in school. Are they glad today that they had a chance to work in your store?"

Margo smiled and answered, "they very much enjoyed working there at the time. It gave them a chance to prove themselves, and to see that they were accepted by adults as authorities. It could only boost their self worth."

I just nodded and went on. "For our teenagers it was a wonderful experience. And there was also another experience that was wonderful for them, and I am sure they will be proud of themselves today, whenever they look back to those years.

In our neighborhood in Denver lived several engineers who worked in the field of rocketry. One of them lived right behind our property, and our son Dieter befriended their son. It took only a short time before Dieter also was bitten by the rocket bug, and decided that designing and building rockets was the thing to do.

There were quite a few teenagers involved in this hobby and many Sundays found us on the large field we called the rocket range. There was a blockhouse, a fenced-in command-and-launch area with twenty remote rocket launchers, two tracking stations 500 feet from the command area, and a public address system for communications. There was even a wind tunnel for testing. The only adult was the range safety officer.

The members developed their own designs and our kitchen table was pressed into service as a design and construction platform. The first live payload rocket originated here. Only paper, glue and balsa wood were allowed in the construction, besides the fabric for the return parachute, which usually resided in a small chamber right behind the nose cone.

There were contests and even national meets where new developments where shown, such as a rocket designed to be fired from the bottom of a 55-gallon drum filled with water. It was demonstrated and it worked.

Those boys and girls really knew what they were doing; and it was also an excellent learning experience. The altitude reached by a rocket had to be calculated from the two azimuth and declination numbers called in from the two tracking stations and Dieter often was part of that team. He had to know geometry; he even could use my five-place logarithm table. I believe this relic is still in his possession.

One of the rockets Dieter had designed was to carry a live payload, a cricket. All went well, except that the cricket suffered some life-threatening damage upon re-entry. Fortunately, Margo always carried a sewing needle someplace on her dress or blouse. This she was forced to donate for a good cause. The next donor was Doris who lost one of her long blond hairs.

Dieter operated on the cricket and the operation was a smashing success. After the cricket was properly sutured it took off in a hurry. And to this day I don't understand why Dieter gave up his promising and successful career as a surgeon and switched to cardiology.

# 54

Let's do another time jump back to 1971, two years after I had resigned from my job. One day we mentioned our search for a suitable business to our paint dealer. His store was in the same shopping center as Margo's first business and he encouraged us to try for a franchise of the Colorado paint manufacturer Komac. We knew that it would be extremely difficult to obtain such a franchise, and it would definitely be beyond our meager financial resources, but it was certainly worth a try.

And so I found myself one day at the reception desk of the Komac factory in Denver, asking the pretty receptionist to announce me to the president of the paint company, a Mr. McLister. I told the receptionist to announce me exactly like this: 'Mr. Schneider is here to see you for a total of exactly six minutes and twenty seconds.' Naturally, this aroused his curiosity and it was not long before I was ushered into his sumptuously appointed office.

After introducing myself I ceremoniously removed my wristwatch and propped it up on the edge of his large mahogany desk so that it was facing me. I then proceeded to tell him why he should have us as a member of his franchise team.

Every once in a while I made it a point to glance at my watch until I came to the end of my speech. Again I looked at my watch and said, 'I see I used up six minutes and ten seconds of your time, you have ten seconds left to say 'yes'. Go ahead, it's your turn now.'

He arose from his chair immediately and with a big smile on his face he shook my hand. 'Welcome to our family,' he boomed, and while still pumping my hand he continued, 'it's people like you we need, people who know how to sell. And you sure did a great job selling me.'

We had not the slightest idea how to run a paint store, but we figured we could learn. First I asked to have the most knowledgeable person walk me through their inventory of items they manufactured, explaining to me their properties, their composition etc. This took all morning till lunchtime and gave me a pretty good grasp of their product line. Fortunately, at that time I still had an extremely long attention span and a good memory for details.

The first hurdle was behind us. Now we had to find a suitable location, not too close to another Komac store, but a site allowing future growth.

Luck was with us. An existing Komac store in Boulder happened to be available. It was unprofitable and was operating in the red; and the inventory was small. So, in 1973, we made a minimum down payment, the remainder to be paid over the next five years, and it was ours.

There was just one hitch. When the first customer walked in and wanted to have a certain color paint, we had to phone the factory since neither of us knew how to add the pigment, each of us assuming that the other knew how to do that.

We worked this business for nine years before selling it in 1982. By this time we had become a wholesaler for Watco products and 3M products. We had branched out to establish another business, Denver Moulding Company, with its own small warehouse in downtown Denver. By now the demand on our time had grown to the point where we just had to make a change.

First we tried taking in a partner, but it did not work out and we had to look for a buyer.

A couple from Chicago finally bought the businesses on a contract and we envisioned ourselves going into retirement with a nice monthly income from the sale of the business. The euphoria lasted about three years, but then the payments started to come in late, and finally stopped. It turned out that the buyer had developed MS and had turned blind. His wife had tried to carry on, but without success, and finally they declared bankruptcy when the government closed in because of back taxes, penalties, and interest. This then was the fourth time we had to start from scratch financially."

"I don't think you counted right, Horst," interrupted Eddy. "I counted as you talked, it's the fifth time. When you came to the States and this one makes two times. Then there was the time you got married. Then two more times; after you got bombed out in Berlin, and finally the currency reform after the war. That's three times. Add two and three together and you get five."

"Ooops, I goofed," I had to admit. "You are right, I forgot the start with the three wooden spoons and the kitchen knife. Sorry.

218

# 55

In 1985 Margo found a small business for sale at half down, with the remainder to be paid over a five-year period. It was located conveniently only two blocks away, just a short walk mornings and evenings. The only hitch was the down payment, we needed twenty-five thousand dollars we didn't have.

Off we went to our trusty bank where we had banked for many years. I explained to the bank president that we still had two unpaid loans with his bank, and that we presently had no income, and that I was 65 years old, but that we needed another loan. He miraculously granted us a twenty-five thousand dollar loan, based on the fact that we had been longtime customers in good standing, and that our business ventures in the past had been successful.

Margo bought the business, a yarn and knitting machine store. There were seven different models of machines on display, and Margo, not knowing anything about them, had to ask those customers who had a particular model, to show her how to operate it. But learn she did and she made enough money to expand.

In the meantime, John, a close friend of ours found a job for me, a job sorting mail at an insurance company where he worked. The job paid minimum wages but that was enough to put bread and butter on the table. The next five years were tough financially, but we managed to pay off the two old bank loans, as well as the loan contract with the former owner. We worked seven days a week, often till after midnight. But it did pay off in the end. We will tell you about that shortly.

But first I want to recount a little story. While I was working at the Equitable Insurance Company in Denver I was having lunch one day with two executives of the company. They commented on the fact that my life had been so full of twists and turns and surprisesm and how dull their lives were in comparison. Then one of them asked the obvious question; why was that so. There is no easy answer I told them, but I could at least provide them with a hint.

I then posed a hypothetical question: what would be your immediate reaction if Saturday night your phone rang and a laughing voice at the other end informed you to get up and be ready in no later that 10 minutes. You looked at the clock and it was a quarter to four in the morning. Now what would you do. The answer was unanimous. - Slam the receiver down and go back to sleep.

And then I told them what happened to us one Sunday morning at a quarter to four. Our phone next to the bed rang persistently. We were told to be ready in 10 minutes. But instead of turning around and going back to sleep, we jumped out of bed, splashed water in our face, combed our hair, and were dressed and ready when the door bell rang. We were hustled into our friend's station wagon and off we drove into the mountains west of Denver, to a beautiful picnic place, overlooking the sleeping city.

We helped unload the supplics and in no time at all the coffee was brewing, blueberry pancakes were bubbling in frying pans, and just as a fiery red sun came over the eastern horizon, the champagne corks popped. What a gorgeous, unforgettable morning, having a blueberry pancake champagne breakfast on the mountainside, while watching a new day being born over the prairie.

The moral of the story: Don't ever say NO to an opportunity to escape the norm.

I remember another night, a Saturday night, when the doorbell rang just past midnight. Outside stood another crazy friend of ours, Gene MacAllister, with whom we had stayed when we came to America. His arms were full of cartons of hot pizza. 'Let's wake up the kids and have a pizza party,' he announced.

We sounded the alarm and soon the kids were milling around the kitchen table, probably more attracted by the aroma of the pizza than our cries of 'wake up, get dressed, and join us in the kitchen.'

Pizza was not the only item being offered it turned out. He also presented us with a big chunk of octopus. The pizza disappeared quickly, but the octopus survived the combined chewing of the whole family. Even Gene was unable to chew off a piece. We finally had to surrender to the fact that it was Octopus One, Schneiders Zero.

These two stories have a small connection with what I want to tell you next.

# 56

But before I go on I think I need my coffee cup refilled," I announced. After a few sips of hot coffee we continued with our story.

"Now back to what I had said about 'paying off'. Our business philosophy had always been to help anytime and in any manner possible and it sure did pay off in 1992.

In 1988 the Sov-US Trading Company, a company dealing with the Soviet Union, had asked us to assist them in designing a floorplan for a plant in Russia, which was to produce knitted items such as sweaters, etc.

They also begged us to assist them in working up a list of equipment they would need, as well as a list of materials, to get them started. However, unfortunately for us, they were going to buy everything directly from the various manufacturers, we were told, so there would be no profit in it for us. But we helped them anyway with their design and their lists.

We did not know at the time that they also had made the rounds in Cleveland, in New York, and in Chicago, as well as in Denver, to find someone to assist them and that they had been turned down everywhere. This we found out much later, when it turned out that the Sov-US Trading Company was financially unable to fulfill the contract they had with Russia.

The Russians had made a sizeable down payment on the contract, but practically all the money had vanished through mismanagement. In fact, the company was on the verge of bankruptcy. Again they came to us for help and asked us to take over the contract.

We stepped in and overhauled the contract. It had been full of errors, omissions, and ambiguities. Neither the Russians, nor the owner of the Sov-US Trading Company, knew much about international trade practices and requirements. It took two years of hard negotiations by phone and fax to get everything cleared up.

Changing the wording of the contract was necessary also because we did not have the finances either to fulfill the contract. But with the contract in its new form and by juggling shipments and bank letters of credit we did succeed.

Juggling the shipment schedules was a major headache since we had to deal with suppliers from many countries: France, Switzerland, Italy, Germany, Great Britain, the US, and Japan.

Meanwhile we also had started to learn some Russian, once a week after work, from eight to ten. As it turned out later, this was a wise move. As a part of the contract we had to fly to Moscow in April 1992 to teach the use of computerized knitting and embroidery machines to a small delegation from the factory, which was located east of the Ural

Mountains.

We had been told that there would be an interpreter available to us. When the young man arrived, we found out that he didn't know anything about knitting or embroidery, but he knew all the latest American movie and music stars. He was no help at all and lasted all of one day.

Before we left for Moscow we bought a whole round cheese, summer sausages, several cans of coffee and all kinds of other staples. The early 1990s were hard times in Russia, everything was in short supply or not available at all. It was like a repeat of the postwar period in Germany. We made a lot of people happy when we later delivered the food we had brought with us to a senior citizen home in Moscow

My first chance to practice my Russian happened right after our arrival at the small old Moscow airport, Sheremedyeva I. Our contact person was nowhere to be seen when we arrived in Moscow and we had no idea where to go or how to get there.

This was the time right after the collapse of the Soviet Union and I went from one end of the airport to the other in a fruitless search for a phone to call our contact. I did find several phones, but the answer was always the same, 'nye rabotayet', which means 'does not work'. But finally we were relieved to see our contact man racing in with a huge bouquet of flowers for Margo, one of the many gallant Russian customs.

He had been given wrong information and had gone to Sheremedyeva II, the newer airport.

However, before he arrived I had gone in search of a phone also on the second floor where there were a number of offices, all with doors shut in typical Russian bureaucratic fashion. It took me some time to locate the Intourist office where I asked the young lady for permission to use her phone. She hardly looked up from her magazine before she managed her answer, which was short and to the point, 'Nyet'.

Before we had left Denver, Margo, with foresight, had collected samples of all kinds of lipstick, body lotion, perfume, etc. When I returned downstairs and told her of the lady's answer, she rummaged around in our luggage and handed me some samples. So fortified I went up the stairs again to the Intourist office where I put my samples on the desk. This time I did not even have to ask for the phone. 'Use the red one,' she said, and then even favored me with a smile."

Bill couldn't contain himself any longer. "You know," he said, "you have told us some of your stories before, but it was always one or two at a time. But now that I hear them together with some more that you have not told us before, your life is beginning to make sense to me. I had always wondered why your life was so full of experiences. It's clear to me now. It has to do with what you call your attitude, or philosophy, or how you approach it.

Gee, I wished I had known you two when I was much younger, maybe some of your attitude would have rubbed off on me. You told us yesterday or the day before that 'Life is a Do-it-yourself Job', and I must say, you did OK. – Sorry I interrupted, I just had to say that. Please go on."

# 57

I nodded. And then a story just popped into my head. I was sure I had not told it before, and since it was funny I decided to tell it now. So I started.

"I have a story, which I did not tell you yet, I think. So, let's do that now. When we lived in Denver we often went elk hunting in the mountains of Colorado. One of the nice rules of our hunting trips with our friends was the rule that Margo was not allowed to do any cooking or cleaning after dinner during our trip. In fact, she almost had to swear an oath not to do any kitchen chores as a condition to accompany the group. She was allowed to tend the fire, even get some firewood, but that was about all she was allowed to do.

On one such hunting trip in the 1970s we camped in the mountains north of Glenwood Springs. On the third day the Radio warned that a sudden and severe winter storm was going to blow in from the north and everyone in our vicinity abandoned their camp to get out of the High Country. Our group was the last to leave, since we had decided to stay till the next day. But for once the weather forecasters were right and we woke up under a blanket of snow almost four inches deep.

Margo and I were sleeping in a small, low Himalaya tent and it took us almost twenty minutes to dig out from under the snow. To make matters worse, Margo had developed laryngitis during the night and could only whisper. And then one of our group put an axe in his foot while chopping firewood, opening a fair sized gash. It was time for us to leave the mountain and get our good friend to the hospital.

The sun had been shining the last few days, and as we approached the half way mark between our camp and the foot of the mountain, we churned up a good amount of mud since this area was exposed to the south. As usual, we were the last car, and so got our fair share of the mud.

When we came to an extremely steep and dangerous downgrade I felt it best to send Margo down another route. She could then join up with me farther down on a shelf road, which was barely wide enough for our car.

I did not have to wait very long before Margo came climbing down the steep hillside on my right to join me. This was not an easy task since she had to enter through the window. But instead of coming in feet first she tried to come in head first. She would have succeeded easily if it had not been for her pants belt getting snagged on the door lock button.

There was about a half-inch of wet muck on the floor, and as I looked on in amazement, her hands slid off the seat and disappeared into the mud. Now Margo was partly inside, but her legs were still uphill outside the car. She turned her face and looked up at me with pleading eyes and whispered hoarsely 'HELP' – 'HELP'. The situation was too comical to stay serious, especially so, since she looked absolutely un-Margo, with her hair in disarray and her face smudged with campfire soot. Both of us started laughing till tears were rolling down our cheeks, which created some startling effects on her sooty face. One of us even wet her pants, and to spare belated embarrassment, I will not reveal who it was. But with lots of pulling and tugging we finally succeeded in getting her inside.

We were still laughing when we arrived at the foot of the mountain and stopped at a gravel pit to clean the windshield, which was encrusted with mud. While I started to scrape the mud from the front of the car, Margo went to the rear to do her part. It took me maybe ten minutes to get all the mud off and I figured that Margo should be about done with the car's backside and I called out to her.

I was right, she was done indeed, but not the way I had figured. While I was slaving away at the front she had cleaned her face, just the front facing part mind you, with some towelettes, then had applied make-up, lipstick and eye shadow.

And as she reappeared I could hardly believe my eyes. Here we had gone hunting way back in the High Country, and Margo being Margo, had smuggled on board a blond wig! From the neck up, in the front at least, she looked as if she was going to the opera. The rest of her still looked like a hobo who had slept in the same boxcar for the last three days.

# 58

In addition to hunting I also very much enjoyed fly-fishing for trout in the cold Colorado streams. One of those was the San Miguel near Telluride in the southwest corner of Colorado.

In the Southwest of Colorado also is a small town called Rico, or at least it used to be small. We often took the road north out of Cortez over the Lizard Head Pass and on to Telluride, passing through this small town. Actually, Rico was not really a town, it was just a place.

But it had its past and many buildings still told of it. The bank building was standing on Main Street, empty and shuttered, the old school house was quiet, and the hotel had not seen guests for many, many years. It was a quaint, quiet place, just one block long.

At the south end was a filling station of sorts. An old-style pump stood in front of a fair-sized but ramshackle wooden building and you could actually buy gasoline there, plus a few other things like candy bars.

Every time we drove through Rico we stopped to say hello to that building's owner, have a cup of coffee with him and swap stories about our lives, his and ours. He had flown solo around the world twice and had the newspaper clippings hanging on the wall to prove it. Raye Benham did not care whether or not you bought gas, or any of the few odd things he sold on occasion, but he loved to have company.

Looking at the structure he lived in one felt almost like leaving an extra quarter for this poor fellow. But poor he was not, he just didn't give a hoot about the trimmings of city life. He seemed to like our company and one day confided in us about his holdings. We were utterly amazed at the amount of real estate, as well as mining claims, he owned.

Later, when we worked at the Mesa Verde Natl. Park we once did go back to Rico. The old filling station was gone, and so was Raye. The new Neon and polished aluminum filling station looked out of place at the south end of town where Raye used to live.

People had moved into town and had started to spruce up the place. The old charm was gone and in its place will probably soon be a traffic signal.

Gone was also another structure we remembered vividly, an outside two-door privy. The first time we noticed it was on a sunny afternoon when a car with New York license plates drove up to the old pump and disgorged a lady. She was dressed as if going to the theater, complete with high heels. She looked utterly out of place.

She asked Raye if she could use what she called a comfort station. He looked at her real close and then told her in his best imitation of a mountain man drawl: 'We ain't got no comfort station or indoor plumbing (which was a lie) but one is welcome to our two-holer. Just make sure to close the door real tight, it has a habit of popping open sometimes.' Pointing at his two-holer he withdrew to the inside of his little store.

With a big mischievous grin he informed us that we would very soon see a real fun spectacle. We watched the lady approaching the two-holer where she hesitated for a moment, eyeing the structure with misgivings and doubt. But then she decided to venture in. She must have been in dire need of, as she called it, a comfort station.

Raye waited a few moments to let her get settled and then grabbed a microphone off the wall and spoke into it: 'Ma'am, would you mind movin' to the other hole, we is paintin' down here.' A few seconds later the door flew open and she shot out of the two-holer as if propelled by a tornado. She ran back to the car as if she wore running shoes instead of high heels. The tires screeched and she was gone.

We laughed so hard that tears were streaming down our cheeks and our tummies hurt. We could visualize the lady trying to find a place to stop and hurriedly disappear behind some bushes. And we wondered for how many years this story would be told in New York City.

Sally had a question for me. "OK, so you knew this guy, but what I want to know is, how do you get to know all those interesting people that Dad said you knew. I mean I want you to explain to me how you got to know him in the first place. There was obviously no reason to stop in this place unless your car broke down."

Now that was a very good question, and an easy one to answer.

"Sally, you should know by now that Margo and I are explorers, we want to know what's out there. So, when we came through Rico the first time, we saw Raye's old place and our curiosity told us to stop and go in.

Next to his door he had some rocks lying around and we bent down to look at them. He came out and asked us if we knew what those rocks were. We told him that, yes, we recognized them right away, they were Jasper. And from there we got into a conversation about minerals, and gems in particular.

He was interesting to listen to and he seemed to think that we were good listeners. I think I just mentioned that he owned quite a few mining claims in the area and so it was natural that we talked about minerals. Anyway, that's how we came to know Raye.

# 59

Let me tell you about another one of our unusual friends, Carlo Creatore. And let me tell you about Carlo's shirt. He and his wife Anna were dear friends of ours for many years. But before I get into the story about Carlo's special shirt I must go back a little in time.

When we had our businesses it was my job to fill out all the myriad government forms. Two of them, the two monthly sales tax reports, were due on the 20th of each month and had to be postmarked with a date no later than the 20th. Being a procrastinator, and working long hours to boot, I usually finished them just in time to drive downtown to the main post office on the 20th late in the evening. On one such late evening I was returning from the post office and decided to drive a different route home. And it was then that I saw a neon sign, which said DANCING. I parked my car to go in and investigate. There were two reasons for me to stop that evening.

The first was the fact that good places to go dancing were hard to find, at least places where they played the dances we liked. Secondly, that evening I had time to explore since Margo was visiting our

Horst Schneider

younger daughter Doris north of Denver and I was therefore in no hurry to return home immediately as I usually did.

When we had our business in Boulder, Colorado, a friend introduced us to the Elks Lodge in town, which had a beautiful, large dance floor where a live band played every weekend, playing just the kind of dance music we favored: Tangos, Cha-chas, Rumbas, Waltzes, Polkas. Practically every Friday and Saturday we left home in the morning with our evening clothes in the car, so we could change after we closed the store and drive to the Elks Club for dinner. Then we danced till the early morning hours, when they closed the Club.

If it was a Friday we grabbed a few hours of sleep and went back to work for another day. If it was a Saturday we usually went to downtown Denver. There a friend of ours was a caretaker of a condo complex, and had the use of the indoor swimming pool at night. After that came breakfast, a few hours of sleep, or not, and we were gone again visiting friends. Even during the week we often went bar hopping, especially if the bar had a piano player. We even struck up some nice friendships with some of the players. At any rate, we lived a fast, full, and happy life, burning our candle at least at two ends, if not three."

Sally looked at me with a mischievous smile. "Then what you are telling us is that hard work and fast living guarantees a long and happy life? Is that right?" she asked.

"Sure is," I told her, "we are the living proof, but let's get on with story, you will have to leave pretty soon.

Finding another place to go dancing closer to home would have been nice. With that in mind I went to investigate the Club 400, as it was called. Inside I found myself in a bar, but there was no dance floor. 'The dance floor is downstairs', answered the bartender when I asked him. Down the stairs I went, and there indeed was a dance floor, but not the kind of dance floor I had been looking for. The band just then came back from their break and started to play and a most shapely young lady appeared from nowhere and started her dance routine.

She was such an accomplished dancer that I didn't even notice, while I watched, that she was shedding one piece of clothing after another as she was dancing. Later we found out that she was from Italy and had studied ballet as a young girl. Then, still a teenager, she had joined a ballet troupe, which toured the Mediterranean states. No wonder she danced like a pro.

One of the dancers was a pretty black lady who later joined me at my little table, and we started to talk. Her name was Michelle. She told me about her young son, I told her about Margo, and we had a good time together. It was late and the club was ready to close but I was not ready to go home yet. So I invited Michelle to join me for a late Chinese dinner. She accepted and phoned her baby sitter that she would be about 45 minutes late. Over dinner we talked some more before the two of us went our separate ways home. When I told Michelle that she would meet Margo as soon as Margo returned, Michelle just laughed.

When Margo came home two days later I told her about my adventure into the dark underworld of striptease dancing, and that I had had dinner with one of the dancers, Michelle. That really aroused her curiosity and that evening found the two of us walking down the stairs to the club. When Michelle saw Margo and me together she alerted the Maitre d', a large, wide shouldered man, to stay close by 'in case we have a jealous and irate wife', he was told.

Soon everyone relaxed after we had invited Michelle to our table. I guess that ours was a rather uncommon occurrence, because we quickly were introduced to some of the other dancers. The Italian, it turned out, was the Maitre d's wife, and while she looked about twenty-six on stage, we later found out that in fact she was over forty. And the big man who had introduced himself as the Maitre d', actually was the Emcee, Carlo Creatore.

We were invited back for a visit. And that night a Wednesday night tradition was born. After the Club 400 closed at night, the dancers, the band, and we, would have breakfast together at a nearby all-night restaurant. That's when we found out that the bandleader was Lena Horne's first husband, and that Precious Diamond was a grandmother with a long career in Las Vegas at $5000 a week.

Once in a while we would change our routine and would join Carlo and his wife for an early Italian Polenta breakfast at their home. And so started our long lasting friendship with Carlo and his wife Anna.

# 60

One of Carlo's better known stage songs was a story about Bruce, a gentleman of a different persuasion. It was the song most requested by Carlo's audience. And it was for this routine that he always had wanted a special stage shirt with a white on white pattern.

Finally Anna and Carlo found just the perfect fabric and Margo volunteered to sew him his special shirt. This was a long introduction to the story I wanted to tell you, but I felt it necessary that you should know the background to why Margo one morning was in her sewing room sewing a shirt.

Right after breakfast Margo was busy getting ready to cut the fabric for Carlo's shirt, which she had promised him for next day's performance. I was in the kitchen working on one of my projects when suddenly a loud wailing could be heard from the sewing room. Moments later Margo came storming out breathing fire. After a few minutes I finally found out that Margo accidentally had cut two identical fronts, instead of a left and a right one.

One cup of coffee later she calmed down and went back to her sewing room to see what she could rescue. Fortunately she had just enough fabric left for another front piece. All went well, except for the sewing machine needle finding her finger and piercing it. This did not get her into a better mood. She quit for a short while, having another cup of coffee, and nursing her finger. Then off she went again to finish Carlo's shirt.

It was quiet for quite a while. But then a loud and unladylike epithet could be heard coming from Margo's sewing room and Margo again stormed out. After she caught her breath, she told me what had happened this time. In her rush to finish the shirt she had accidentally sewn the right sleeve into the left armhole. After a while and another cup of coffee, she recovered and went back to finish the shirt.

There was one more episode, which I will bypass. I will only mention that it did not improve Margo's mood one iota.

But when the shirt was finished we admired it. It was not just beautiful, it was absolutely stunning, and we knew that Carlo would be overjoyed. Margo had proudly hung it on the top of the doorframe at the kitchen entrance. There it resided while Margo prepared dinner and there it peacefully stayed through half of the dinner. But then our peaceful dinner was interrupted by Margo's loud and anguished groans of 'NO, NO'.

She had sewn the front like a girl's blouse, right to left. I thought it was just right for Carlo's song about Bruce and I said so, christening it Carlo's Brucie shirt. After all Bruce was of a different persuasion. This statement almost had me evicted from the dinner table.

There is not much more to report, except that Carlo absolutely adored his new Brucie shirt. Margo had extricated herself from her dilemma by making a false front, which looked just right on Carlo's stage shirt.

# 61

We could finally retire in 1993, at the age of 73, after we came back from Russia. We were finished with our obligations, we had fulfilled the contract, and we had enough money left over to pay off the down payment loan at the bank.

For a long time our plan had been to eventually trade in our fifth wheel for a motor home, sell the house, and travel footloose and fancy-free. And 1993 was year we finally made it a reality.

In 1996 we made one more trip to Europe, one week in St. Petersburg, one in Moscow, four weeks in Germany, and one week in France.

We were accompanied to Europe by another couple. We had promised them some time in the past that they would be welcome to accompany us should we ever fly back to Germany. We had known these friends for 25 years and they thought we might make good guides. Also, we could share lots of expenses, such as car rental and gasoline, toll charges, etc. This was a most enjoyable trip for all concerned.

We had sold our house in Schimmeldewog to a relative of my father's wife and they let us stay at the old house for several days. From there we took side trips to Heidelberg, to the old medieval town of Rothenburg, to Creglingen's Herrgottskirche, a medieval church dating to 1383 and containing one of the altars of the famous German woodcarver Tilmann Riemenschneider.

In Russia we spent one week in the beautiful city of St. Petersburg, making daily excursions to castles, museums, etc. Another week was spent in Moscow where we had rented a furnished three room apartment. We went shopping for groceries like the Russians and the ladies cooked as if we were at home in America.

While Margo and I did not want to go to Paris, our friends just had to see that city. But what could we do, we just had to grant them their wish. Driving our car in Paris was as crazy as I remembered from prior visits, so we decided to stay in a hotel on the outskirts. We found a nice hotel in LeBourget, northeast of Paris, near the old Paris airport. There we settled in for a few days.

One more memorable event happened on our way back from Paris to Germany. As was our custom in Europe, we had bought some French bread, some cheese, and some sausage, and had lunch in the car while traveling. Before we left our hotel Margo had thoughtfully picked up some small wet towelettes the hotel had provided, so that we could wash our hands after lunch. They were perfumed in a very unusual way, and it was not until I asked for the wrapper that I found out we had wiped our hands with clear shoe polish.

Otherwise there is not much to report about our trip. Except maybe our experience on the night before the last in Germany. We always stayed in small villages where the butcher usually rented out a room or two, and so we stopped at a real small out of the way place. They didn't have a butcher, or any kind of store for that matter, since they just traded with each other, a sort of self-sufficient little place. But they did have a bistro with a few tables and chairs.

Yes, replied the lady owner, she had a room for rent, but it had only one small bed. Next year she said, she would have another room, which was still under construction. Then she let slip that there was already some carpet on the floor, and there was a bed of sorts. This, we told her, was all we needed.

'Yes', she said,' you could have it if it wasn't for the fact that this room is under the roof, sort of a mansard room and that we don't have stairs in place yet'. Then she added 'but there is a ladder you could use'.

We decided to take the room even after she added one more bit of news: 'There is no toilet, either, - but I can give you a bucket'.

We did use the ladder, but we didn't use the bucket.

The lady redeemed herself the next morning with a scrumptious breakfast. After we were finished she almost physically forced eleven glasses of homemade jams and jellies on us. We tried to decline. But nothing helped. Not even when we explained that we couldn't possibly take all that loot with us on the airplane. We finally divided the loot between us, and in the end we somehow managed to get everything stowed away in our suitcases. The glasses even arrived in Denver in one piece.

This was our last trip to Europe.

# 62

As I said, we finally had paid off all our bills and loans, bought a motor home, and now were ready to sell our house.

Naturally, much had to be done to the house before it could be put on the market. We painted, we hammered, we scrubbed. And at that time I again became intimately acquainted with St. Nepomuk.

I must have been around five or six years old when I first became acquainted with St. Nepomuk when I lived with my uncle in Saarbrücken. Despite the fact that I was not catholic I could not help learning much about Catholicism since it was the region's predominant religion. As a non-Catholic you had to have a smattering of knowledge of their ways if you wanted go through life unharmed.

St. Nepomuk is one of the lesser Saints. He was, or is, the protector of bridges and also was reputed to make lost items invisible if properly invoked by prayer. This I found out when I heard one family friend telling my uncle that St. Nepomuk had helped her find the ring she had lost on the bridge across the river. 'He sat on the ring so no one could see it,' she said, and then continued: 'this was now the second time he helped me, so you know it must be true. As a friend I really wished you could see the light and come with me to our church.'

I have thought of St. Nepomuk many times since then, especially now that I am getting a bit older. I also have found out that he will work even if I do not evoked him by prayer.

While I was busy nailing, drilling, sawing, and painting to spruce up our house for sale, I thought of St. Nepomuk often. Especially once when I absolutely could not locate my drill for over a week. When I finally found it, the drill was so well hidden under some plywood pieces that I had to assume a higher power was at work. Who else could it have been but St. Nepomuk, I reasoned.

Having things become invisible in broad daylight has become much more frequent lately. Just last week I was frantically looking for my pen, which I had laid on my desk at the usual place. It was not there. I walked though the house looking at other likely places, but no luck. I checked my desk a second time; the pen was not to be seen. Margo finally helped me and found it right where it belonged on my desk and where I had looked twice before. Maybe St. Nepomuk, being a less well known Saint, enjoys having a little fun with me once in a while."

Eddy spoke up and said, "you can't be serious about that Nepomuk fellow, I never heard of him. Are you sure you got the name right?"

"Sure I am sure," I answered him. "He was born in Bohemia. You can look him up on the Internet, I did. He is a genuine Saint.

# 63

At any rate we had bought our motor home before we sold the house so we would have a place to stay while we worked on the house. Also, we wanted to get used to living in a motor home. We were looking forward to traveling the USA, footloose and fancy-free, being retired, and not having a care in the world.

As it turned out we traveled for two summers, and during the winter we stayed in the Arizona desert, just 15 miles north of Yuma. But we felt the need to be active, and after two years of travel we started to work as volunteers at the Mesa Verde Natl. Park during the summer until we finally bought a prefab house on the outskirts of Yuma in 2000.

All of this was in the future and at the moment we didn't know about any of it yet. Right now we only knew that we had to get ready to sell the house. And before we could do that we had to clean it out.

We collected myriad of items we had no intention of keeping and earmarked them for a huge yard sale in our driveway. In fact, this sale went on for three weekends. We were utterly amazed at how much unnecessary stuff we had managed to collect and store in forty years of living in the same place.

The yard sale was a tremendous success, people stopped and pawed through the stuff we displayed. Quite a few of the usable items were sold quickly. There were several tables of discards and people actually gave us money for some things they probably will have in their yard sale some years in the future.

There was one particular box that I enjoyed watching, or rather I watched the reactions of the ladies who opened it. Many women closed it immediately and shot some furtive glances left and right with the expression clearly written on their faces: 'I hope no one saw me looking inside this box'.

Some looked and then straightened up with rightful indignation and the expression of 'Well, I never would have believed it', and then marched off to their car without looking back. A few smiled conspiratorially and sometimes called their husbands for an exchange of a few whispered words.

But this item just did not sell. At least not until day six, the final day of the sale, when a lady picked up the box, looked inside and then almost shouted, 'I always wanted those'.

She must have been the happiest customer we had had, thanking us profusely for, as she said, making her day. She danced back to her car and her waiting husband, triumphantly waving her catch, but we could see that she refused to show him her purchase.

What I just told you was actually the end of the story. So let me now start at the beginning.

Years ago I had been looking for these items in

the box for quite some time since Margo had dropped several hints about wanting some. But I had no success until one day when I discovered a specialty store in North Denver carrying theatrical supplies, costumes, props etc. On a hunch I walked in and told the saleslady of my unsuccessful search.

'No problem,' she said, and led me to a counter where there were neatly displayed at least a dozen of them. I selected two, a gold pair and a red pair, with matching tassels.

'What kind of swivels do you want with them', asked the lady, to which I could only reply that I had not the foggiest idea.

'Well then, is the lady a professional,' she wanted to know. 'Not really', I answered, 'I am buying them as a birthday gift for my wife.'

And after I had paid for my purchase she stopped me at the door saying, 'I so wished that more husbands would do that, but in six years of working here you are the first one. I am proud of you. Enjoy.' She then shook my hand, and I was on my way home.

I waited until Margo's birthday to present her with my precious gift, and was she ever surprised. But then my gift disappeared and I did not see it any more until about three weeks later. And now it was my turn to be surprised. In just three weeks my wife had become a master of the art."

Sally started laughing, clapped her hands and turned to her husband. "You see," she told him, "this is how to properly treat a wife. Just imagine what you have missed out on."

We all joined in her merriment, although I had the impression that Helen, being the youngest of the group, felt just a bit uncomfortable. But this was a fun ending to our story, because I was not willing to 'talk story' any longer tonight.

At any rate, I knew that Eddy was getting antsy. He had told me that he still had a little packing to do, and he certainly did not want to arrive at he airport late.

We all got up, stretched our legs for a moment and then said our good-byes, Sally hugging Margo and whispering something into Margo's ear that I could not hear. It must have been funny because both women giggled and grinned from ear to ear.

The two guys and I shook hands. They thanked us for a very interesting and entertaining evening and turned to leave.

Helen lingered for a moment and then turned to me, put an arm around my shoulder and said in a low voice, "please forgive me for my outburst yesterday. It just goes to show how sheltered my live is. So sheltered that I had a hard time understanding the times you lived through. But Dad and I had a good talk last night after we came home. I think I understand now. I am sorry." Then she gave me a sincere hug and turned to follow her family to their car.

This and other quality books are available from

# OverLookedBooks

Visit us online at:
www.overlookedbooks.com

Printed in the United States
35706LVS00003B/115-141

9 781595 940230